Land Your
Dream Job

52 Brilliant Ideas

one good idea can change your life

Land Your Dream Job

High-Performance Techniques to Get Noticed, Get Hired, and Get Ahead

John Middleton, Ken Langdon, and Nikki Cartwright

A Perigee Book

A PERIGEE BOOK
Published by the Penguin Group
Penguin Group (USA) Inc.
375 Hudson Street, New York, New York 10014, USA
Penguin Group (Canada), 90 Eglinton Avenue East, Suite 700, Toronto, Ontario M4P 2Y3, Canada
(a division of Pearson Penguin Canada Inc.)
Penguin Books Ltd., 80 Strand, London WC2R 0RL, England
Penguin Group Ireland, 25 St. Stephen's Green, Dublin 2, Ireland (a division of Penguin Books Ltd.)
Penguin Group (Australia), 250 Camberwell Road, Camberwell, Victoria 3124, Australia
(a division of Pearson Australia Group Pty. Ltd.)
Penguin Books India Pvt. Ltd., 11 Community Centre, Panchsheel Park, New Delhi—110 017, India
Penguin Group (NZ), 67 Apollo Drive, Rosedale, North Shore 0632, New Zealand
(a division of Pearson New Zealand Ltd.)
Penguin Books (South Africa) (Pty.) Ltd., 24 Sturdee Avenue, Rosebank, Johannesburg 2196,
South Africa

Penguin Books Ltd., Registered Offices: 80 Strand, London WC2R 0RL, England

While the authors have made every effort to provide accurate telephone numbers and Internet addresses at the time of publication, neither the publisher nor the authors assume any responsibility for errors, or for changes that occur after publication. Further, the publisher does not have any control over and does not assume any responsibility for author or third-party websites or their content.

LAND YOUR DREAM JOB

Portions from *High Impact CVs* copyright © 2005 by The Inifinite Ideas Company Limited
Portions from *Knockout Interview Answers* copyright © 2005 by The Inifinite Ideas Company Limited
Cover art by Corbis
Cover design by Liz Sheehan
Text design by Baseline Arts Ltd., Oxford

First American omnibus edition: November 2007
High Impact CVs was originally published in Great Britain in 2005 by The Infinite Ideas Company Limited.
Knockout Interview Answers was originally published in Great Britain in 2005 by The Infinite Ideas Company Limited.

Perigee trade paperback ISBN: 978-0-399-53369-3

PRINTED IN THE UNITED STATES OF AMERICA

10 9 8 7 6 5 4 3 2 1

Most Perigee books are available at special quantity discounts for bulk purchases for sales promotions, premiums, fund-raising, or educational use. Special books, or book excerpts, can also be created to fit specific needs. For details, write: Special Markets, Penguin Group (USA) Inc., 375 Hudson Street, New York, New York 10014.

Brilliant ideas

Brilliant features

Each chapter of this book is designed to provide you with an inspirational idea that you can read quickly and put into practice right away.

Throughout you'll find four features that will help you get right to the heart of the idea:

- *Try another idea* If this idea looks like a life-changer then there's no time to lose. *Try another idea* will point you straight to a related tip to expand and enhance the first.

- *Here's an idea for you* Give it a try—right here, right now—and get an idea of how well you're doing so far.

- *Defining ideas* Words of wisdom from masters and mistresses of the art, plus some interesting hangers-on.

- *How did it go?* If at first you do succeed try to hide your amazement. If, on the other hand, you don't this is where you'll find a Q and A that highlights common problems and how to get over them.

Introduction

Question: Who's more likely to be invited to an interview? An outstanding performer with an average resumé or an average performer with an outstanding resumé?

When you're going for a new job, you may well be in competition with hundreds of other people. It's therefore vital for your resumé to distinguish itself from the rest of the pack.

This is harder than it sounds. I've read literally tens of thousands of resumés in my time and most of them were mind-numbingly, teeth-grindingly dull. The vast majority of resumés in circulation today make ditchwater seem comparatively interesting and redefine watching paint dry as an extreme sport for adrenaline junkies.

It's a curious thing, but when it comes to describing ourselves on paper, perfectly competent and interesting people with excellent career track records somehow manage to portray themselves as bland nonentities. To put it politely, most people have uncompelling resumés. Only a handful of us have figured out that a resumé is a one-to-one marketing document, not a desiccated litany of turgid facts. But let's face it, whichever of the two camps we fall into, there's room for improvement.

And that's where this book comes in. Look at this book as a series of prods and prompts that add up to a comprehensive resumé health check. Some of the 52 ideas are action-oriented. Others are more reflective. All are designed to get you thinking about how you can improve the positive impact of your resumé.

Once you've found the right job opportunity, and sent in your immaculately prepared resumé, all that's left to land the working life of your dreams is to win at the interview. The art of successful interviews includes the art of interesting and free-flowing conversation. It's also about technique—techniques for interviewing and techniques for being interviewed. Here's how to bone up on great answers to the interviewers' questions, and to make sure you understand exactly what they're looking for.

Despite scientific advances in hiring techniques such as assessment centers and psychometric testing (if you don't know now, you'll know what they are when you've read the relevant chapters), the interview remains the main way that managers decide which people they invite to work for them. It's an interesting struggle, the one between interviewee and interviewer, in that both sides can win. The hiring company can get the right person and the candidate can get a job that they are right for and that is right for them.

But it's competitive, of course. In most interview situations there are other people competing for the same job. Beating them off means thinking about and rehearsing good answers to the most popular questions that'll be thrown at you. This book covers all the standard questions you're likely to be asked and suggests prize-winning answers. And then it does a bit more.

We'll talk about being scrupulously honest, but we'll also show you how to give that honesty the best possible spin. We'll look at exploiting your strengths and putting your weaknesses into a context where not only do they not matter, but by the end of the interview they may very well have morphed into strengths. After all, though everyone wants a win/win result, the point of going to an interview is to be offered the job. So, yes, you need to be open so that they see the real you; but, yes, you need a bit of guile as well to put you out in front as the candidate with what it really takes.

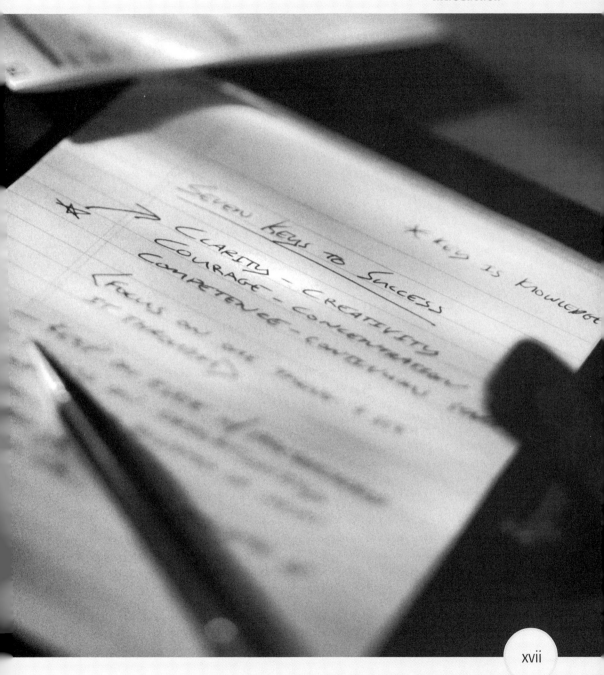

High-Impact Resumés

1

Dream a little dream

High-impact resumés reflect precisely what you're looking to achieve from your career. So, before putting pen to paper, consider what you want from the work you do.

As a child, what did you want to be when you grew up? Moreover, how do you presently feel about your career? Is it moving along nicely? Going well but not well enough? Stalled?

Here are twelve questions that are designed to help you get a handle on the state of your career. Don't feel you have to answer each question in painstaking detail; simply go for those that seem the most relevant or intriguing.

1. In what elements of your career have you been most successful? And least successful?

2. What aspects of your career have you enjoyed the most? And the least?

3. More specifically, what has been the most satisfying role you have undertaken to date?

Here's an idea for you...

Make a list of the constraints affecting your career choices over the next few years. These may include financial issues, qualifications, where you live and work, your ability to relocate, and so on. Make a brief note of how important each constraint is.

4. With the benefit of 20/20 hindsight, are there any points in your career or life where you would have made a different choice or decision?

5. How do you feel when you get up to go to work in the morning?

6. What aspects of your current job do you enjoy the most? And the least?

7. Do you enjoy working with others?

8. How are you regarded by the people you work with?

9. Do subordinates, peers, and senior managers hold different views about you? If so, what conclusions can you draw from this?

10. Have you had a new boss recently, say, in the last two years? If so, what impact has this had on the way you feel?

11. How ambitious are you these days?

12. What do you want out of the work you do? Are you getting it?

THE BIG THREE CAREER OPTIONS

Unless you want to retire, downshift, start your own business, or continue as you are (in which case why are you reading this book?), here are your three main career options:

New role in the same organization

Internal career development can be an excellent way of moving into new fields and learning new skills. Because this option involves staying in your current organization, you wouldn't have the distraction of having to absorb a new culture or a different set of operating principles. You would also know who's who. If you're unhappy with your current work discipline, this can be a good way for you to find a more suitable area.

Similar role in a new organization

This is perhaps the easiest proposition to take to the external job marketplace, as employers tend to be fairly conservative when assessing who they want to join their company. If they're looking for a finance director and you're already the finance director of a similar enterprise, you're much more likely to succeed than a finance manager from a completely different sector who's looking for a promotion.

Try another idea...

Got all you need to start putting a resumé together? Take a look at IDEA 3, *What's your type?*, which will help you choose the best format.

Defining idea...

"Optimism is a strategy for making a better future. Because unless you believe that the future can be better, it's unlikely you will step up and take responsibility for making it so. If you assume that there is no hope, you guarantee that there will be no hope."
NOAM CHOMSKY, quoted in *Wired*

3

Defining Idea...

"Ah, there's nothing more exciting than science. You get all the fun of sitting still, being quiet, writing down numbers, paying attention. Science has it all."
PRINCIPAL SEYMOUR SKINNER, from *The Simpsons*

New role in a new organization

Hard on the heels of the easiest proposition to take to the external job marketplace is the hardest proposition. It *is* possible to change career direction and companies at the same time, but you'll need to work hard at it and be very convincing and persuasive about (a) why you're trying to make the move and (b) your ability to perform the new role effectively.

PAUSE FOR THOUGHT

Taking stock of your career is not a five-minute exercise. Neither is deciding what you want to do next. So, let's imagine we can hear a number of harp arpeggios with reverb to denote the passage of time…

ENLIGHTENMENT

I take it you've decided what you want to do next and you're going to need a resumé? Excellent. Now let's get going.

Q **I've been examining my career, but I'm struggling with the self-examination. Why should I bother?**

How did it go?

A *You're not alone. Most of us never get around to asking ourselves some fairly fundamental questions about the work we do and whether we've found our niche. Taking stock of our career to date is important, however, because it'll point to how content we currently are and whether we need to take some form of remedial action.*

Q **I can cope with looking back over my career because at least there's something concrete to explore, but how can I come to grips with questions like "What do you want out of the work you do? Are you getting it?"**

A *To give some shape to your thinking, you may find it helpful to note what you want under the following ten headings:*

1. ***Money**: e.g., how much are you looking to earn?*

2. ***Working hours**: e.g., how many would you like to work? Nine to five or non-standard? How much vacation would you like?*

3. ***Job security**: e.g., how important is it to you?*

4. ***Level of challenge**: e.g., do you prefer to operate within a comfort zone or to be really stretched?*

5. ***Type of work**: e.g., manual or knowledge-based?*

5

6. **Independence**: e.g., working with other people or alone?

7. **Management responsibility**: e.g., do you welcome or hate it?

8. **Technical competence**: e.g., do you have or would you like a specialized skill?

9. **Work–life balance**: e.g., how important is it? Considering downshifting?

10. **Location**: e.g., indoors or outdoors? City or country? This country or abroad?

You should have a much better picture of your career aspirations once you've gathered your thoughts under these headings.

2

Eight potentially life-changing seconds

On average, it takes eight seconds to decide whether to continue reading a resumé or to trash it. Here's how to capture and keep the reader's attention in those first vital moments.

At the risk of upsetting Fahrenheit 9/11 director Michael Moore, I'd like to propose that anybody about to write their resumé should give a tip of their hat to Tony Blair and George W. Bush.

In recent times, prime ministers and presidents have placed great emphasis on the impact they can make during their first 100 days in office. It's a period of heightened interest for the media and the voters, and a good strong launch can create a positive impetus for the remainder of their term of office. The same principles apply when you're putting together your resumé. So, how do you go about grabbing and holding the reader's attention in those first eight seconds?

"Time is money."
BENJAMIN FRANKLIN

Defining
idea...

Here's an idea for you...

Read your profile statement out loud to yourself. Is the language as natural as possible? There's a tendency for profile statements to be jam-packed with managerial gobbledygook and clichés. So, no "proactive self-starter" nonsense, please. That said, you do want to be upbeat and positive about yourself.

The fact is, if you can't convince the reader that you're well worth an interview by the time they're midway down page one of your resumé, it's unlikely they'll read much farther. Think of the first half of page one as your prime selling space. Your aim should be to try to feature all of your major arguments for being interviewed in that space.

Writing a resumé isn't like writing a novel, where you slowly tease and intrigue the reader, building gradually to a compelling climax. With a resumé, your impact must be front-end loaded. There's no point in introducing a new and compelling piece of information halfway down the second page of your resumé, as chances are the reader won't reach that point and so it won't be noticed.

So, what's the best information to put on that first half page? Well, virtually all recruiters expect to see your name and contact details at the top of the first page. Not just your name, address, and home telephone number, by the way. You should also include your cell phone number and an email address, as these are good indicators of your technological literacy.

Defining idea...

"When I've got, say, fifty or sixty resumés to look through, I simply don't have time to go through them all in detail."
JOHN VILLIS, recruitment manager

After your contact details, I'd recommend including a two- or three-line profile statement. We'll go into more detail about profiles elsewhere, but for now think of it as a sixty- to eighty-word précis of what you have to offer that would make you a prime contender for the position you're going for.

By the time you've included contact details and a profile statement, you should still have around a half to two-thirds of that first half page still available to you. What follows the profile will vary according to what elements of your background and experience most closely match what the recruiter is looking for. If they're trying to recruit somebody who can do A, B, and C, then you'll need to show explicit evidence of your attainments and experience at doing A, B, and C. If this evidence can best be shown in your current/most recent role, then you'll probably want to go straight into your career history. If, on the other hand, you need to draw on your broader career and experience to prove your competence at A, B, and C, a section called something like "Key Achievements" or "Key Skills and Experience" would suit your purpose better.

The recruiter is only likely to read on beyond this first portion of your resumé if they're convinced you explicitly meet the specification they're recruiting against. This is therefore not the time for subtlety. Above all, don't rely on the recruiter to draw inferences from the information you provide. Concentrate on filling that first half page with as much relevant information as you can, paying particular attention to addressing the job and person requirements that the recruiter has stated. Given this, it goes without saying that to feature a piece of information that the recruiter is likely to regard as irrelevant is a definite no-no.

Once you've got your profile statement together, think about your elevator pitch. More about that in IDEA 22, *Perfect your personal elevator pitch.*

Try another idea...

"Time is precious, but truth is more precious than time."
BENJAMIN DISRAELI

Defining idea...

9

How did it go?

Q   Is eight seconds for real? I didn't realize recruiters were quite that lazy!

A   *Pretty much. Some studies suggest that the figure could be as low as three seconds, but no more than thirty seconds max on average. It's pragmatism as opposed to laziness in my view. Do the math. A typical advertisement in the Sunday papers pulls in around 500 applications. Realistically, if there's one post to fill, then eight to ten interviewees should do the trick, with maybe half a dozen candidates in reserve. The recruiter's challenge is therefore to whittle the applications down from 500 to 15 as quickly and fairly as possible. Allowing two minutes per resumé would mean over two days spent going through them all. Besides, when they're in a position to eliminate 97 percent of the applicants, they can set high standards for making the shortlist. They can also afford to reject candidates for relatively minor reasons.*

Q   When companies are shortlisting on that basis, how can they be sure they're getting the best candidates?

A   *They can't. The process is designed to pick up those people who convey succinctly and explicitly how they meet the selection criteria. The candidate who might be the best in reality yet doesn't convey their proposition effectively is always in danger of missing out.*

3

What's your type?

The two main types of resumés in circulation are the reverse chronological and the functional. They can both work extremely well, but which to use and when?

One of the more important decisions to make concerning your resumé is how to structure the information you want to present. There are many variations on a theme, but the decision really boils down to one of two options.

Let's have a quick look at each in turn:

THE REVERSE CHRONOLOGICAL RESUMÉ

This type of resumé details your education and the jobs you've held in sequence. The most effective use of a chronological resumé is to list your experience in reverse order, i.e., starting with your current or most recent role and then moving back in time, and then treating your education in the same way.

Here's an idea for you... **Produce your resumé in a different format from the one you normally use and compare the two. You might surprise yourself with how good the alternate version looks. Then consider experimenting with a format that mixes both styles.**

The standard layout would be as follows:

Part One   Contact details (name, address, telephone numbers, email)

Part Two   Profile statement

Part Three   Career history (providing the most detail about your most recent role, with previous roles taking up progressively less space)

Part Four   Education and training/professional qualifications (also in reverse chronological order, so that you're emphasizing your most recent attainments)

Part Five   Interests (try to give examples that suggest a good mixture of positive qualities like leadership, personal fitness, intellectual capability, etc.)

The main benefit of a chronological layout is that the first page of your resumé features prominently, your most recent (and typically most senior) role. Remember, you only have seconds to grab the attention of the person reading your resumé, so you want to make sure that you get all your big-hitting points across early.

There are some drawbacks to the chronological resumé, however, notably that:

- If you're a job-hopper, this type of resumé will display that very graphically.
- Any gaps in your career history are likely to stand out.
- Your skills and achievements may not be signaled clearly to the reader if they're spread over a number of the roles you've held.
- If your most recent role is a different type of role from the one you've applied for, this may instill doubt into the mind of the reader.

That said, the chronological resumé is still by far the most widely used format. In fact, it's reckoned that around 80–90 percent of resumés in circulation follow the chronological format. Moreover, the vast majority of recruitment managers prefer to see a candidate's information in this format.

Achievements are important, but so is your softer side. Try IDEA 16, _My hobbies are Ping-Pong, playing the ukulele, and going to the theater_, for tips on how to get your broader interests across.

Try another idea...

"It is not enough to do your best; you must know what to do, and then do your best."
W. EDWARDS DEMING

Defining idea...

13

THE FUNCTIONAL RESUMÉ

This type of resumé is organized by skill rather than job title. It pays no heed to chronology and instead focuses on the individual's skills and abilities that are relevant to the role applied for. Examples of areas that might be relevant are leadership, project management, customer service, and so on.

The functional resumé can be productive if your most recent career history isn't particularly indicative of future direction. The main drawbacks are that it's more time-consuming to draw up and that people more used to seeing "traditional" chronological resumés sometimes regard it with a degree of suspicion.

EMPHASIZE YOUR ACHIEVEMENTS

Whichever format you decide to go with, make sure you concentrate on what you've achieved in your various roles and where you've made a positive difference. Don't simply produce a series of generic job descriptions. The focus should be less on the nitty-gritty of your job responsibilities and more on your personal impact.

Q **I'm still struggling to understand when to use a chronological or a functional resumé. Can you help?**

How did it go?

A *The chronological resumé draws the recruiter's attention to your recent job history and experience. It therefore works particularly well when you're looking to continue in the same type of role and industry. It also enables you to highlight a steady progression in your field. For the more traditional employers, it's the format they're most familiar and comfortable with. The functional resumé draws attention to the skills and strengths you've amassed over the course of your career. It works well when you want to make a significant career change because it puts the emphasis on your transferable skills. If you've been with one employer for a long time, it can usefully shift attention toward all the skills you've acquired in the role and averts it away from your single employer. On the other side of the coin, focusing on skills and experience can take the edge off a history of frequent job-hopping.*

Q **Which type of resumé is currently in fashion?**

A *The best resumé to use will vary according to circumstances, but a chronological resumé that also gives some examples of achievements in each role will hold up to scrutiny. It's also important to remember that the chronological and functional formats are only two basic templates. There's no reason why you shouldn't create a hybrid of the two if you feel it gets your proposition across more compellingly.*

15

4

Cut to the chase

Score points with the reader for every line of your resumé and concentrate on identifying your high-value content.

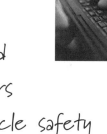

Your resumé shouldn't be an unexpurgated account of your life to date. Recruiters simply won't be interested in that bicycle safety badge you earned at the age of ten.

When a recruiter tells you that your resumé is "comprehensive," it's not always a compliment. The better your resumé is edited and the more it focuses on the particular needs of the job you're going for, the better your chances of getting an interview.

Here are a few tips on how to play the various sections of your resumé:

EXPERIENCE

When you provide details of the jobs you've held, the main areas you need to focus on for each role are:

- Your position, the organization where you work(ed), and the relevant dates

Here's an idea for you...

Try this test on the first draft of your resumé. Highlight in green the lines you think positively sell you against the specific vacancy you're applying for. Use yellow to highlight any "neutral" information that neither sells nor harms you. And then red for anything that the recruiter might consider negative or problematic. What does the balance of shadings tell you?

- An outline of responsibilities and accountabilities

- Your personal and managerial skills

- Any significant achievements

Once you've compiled all this information, you should ask yourself three key questions:

1. Is this information relevant to the needs of the reader?

2. Does it provide positive evidence of my skills and competence?

3. Does this information add value?

EDUCATION AND QUALIFICATIONS

Don't automatically trot out every single qualification you hold. Judge how much detail the reader is likely to be interested in, given the job you're going for. For example, if you're applying to be Director of Finance in a blue-chip company, chances are that the grade you got in your woodworking exam twenty years ago isn't going to be one of your most impressive trump cards. On the other hand, it would be extremely relevant if you want to be considered for a carpentry apprenticeship.

GENERAL

Eliminate unnecessary headings

For example, there's no need to put "Resumé" at the top of your resumé. Besides stating the obvious, it takes up valuable space that you could devote to making a selling point.

Keep it short

As far as possible, stick to two sheets of paper, single sided. Resumés are subject to the whims of changing taste, but right now long and detailed resumés are definitely out of fashion. Besides, keeping it short forces you to be concise and relevant.

Use active verbs

Just compare the punch of active verbs like "implemented," "launched," and "optimized" with the rather more mundane "maintained," "administered," "recorded," and even "managed." Active verbs will give your resumé more zip and impact.

Stuff to leave out

As a rule, don't include:

- The reason(s) why you're leaving your current job

- The salary you're looking for

- References

For what *not* to include in your resumé, take a look at IDEA 10, *The seven deadly resumé sins.*

Try another idea...

"He knew the precise psychological moment when to say nothing."
OSCAR WILDE, *The Picture of Dorian Gray*

Defining idea...

19

- Political allegiances

- Pre-college education

- The months when you changed/started jobs (just the years will do)

- A photograph

There's an acid test to apply when deciding what to put in and what to leave out. Go through your resumé and ask yourself whether each piece of information makes it more likely that you'll be invited to interview. Some pieces of information are neutral but necessary, such as your name and contact details, but the vast majority of the content should be positive and relevant.

Q **I've tried that three-color exercise you suggested and I have a balance of around 50 percent green, 40 percent yellow, and 10 percent red. Now what do I do?**

How did it go?

A *Here's a clue. Unless your first page is predominantly green following your contact details, you're unlikely to get short-listed.*

Q **OK, got that. Anything else?**

A *Well, the best resumés I've seen have a mix of around 80 percent green, 20 percent yellow, and 0 percent red. The first issue you need to address is that red percentage. Given that this is your marketing document, to have 10 percent of your resumé going against you is bad news. Actually, it's disastrous news if there's anything highlighted in red on page one. So, first delete all the red parts. Next, look at the amount of yellow material you have. The only yellow sections you should have are your contact details (your location may be a green factor, but let's not get too picky), maybe some elements of your personal details, possibly some stages of your early career, and, lastly, any qualifications and training that might not connect directly to the job you're going for. Decide what proportion of that yellow stuff is vital and delete the rest. Chances are you now have lots more valuable space open for green business, so build in some more achievements for starters.*

21

5

Learn to speak "behaviorese"

Use your resumé as a tool to illustrate your competencies and you'll really impress the recruiters.

Many organizations now have competency systems in place, sometimes covering just the key roles in the organization but often embracing every job.

Broadly speaking, competencies are skills or characteristic actions used by individuals to enable them to cope successfully with a variety of situations both within and outside of work. In a nutshell, they define the skills and behaviors that are directly related to superior performance in a given role.

Alongside all the organizations that have competency systems, most professions have come up with their own set of competency standards. And not just the obvious professions. In 1999, for example, the British Standards Institution published a professional standard for nightclub bouncers.

Keep a behavioral log in which you can record behavioral evidence on a regular basis. This will put you in a good position when it's time to update your resumé or fill in an application form in the future.

Although the headings change from company to company and from profession to profession, the following are some of the most commonly found competency elements:

Achievement drive	Judgment
Analytical thinking	Leadership
Business integrity	Networking
Business knowledge	Openness to ideas
Change orientation	People development
Communicating and influencing	Planning and organization
Contribution to results	Preference for action
Creative thinking	Problem solving
Customer focus	Professionalism
Decision making	Self-confidence
Facilitation	Strategic thinking
Financial management	Teamwork
Handling information	Technical knowledge
Innovation	Tenacity
Interpersonal sensitivity	Thinking skills

If you work or have worked in an environment that uses a competency system, you'll know that they're regularly used to support recruitment and performance monitoring, as well as training and development activity.

There's more on interpreting job postings in IDEA 6, *Reading the runes.*

Try
another
idea…

These days most job postings explicitly identify the competencies that the successful candidate will need to have. Just to take a couple of examples from a weekend paper, one advertisement for a managing director refers to the need for, amongst other things, a high level of skill in the following: team building, change management, results orientation, and a hands-on mentality. Another job calls for someone with integrity, robustness, analytical skills, and a gift for leadership.

Anybody wishing to apply for either of those jobs would need to be able to demonstrate a proven capability in these competency areas. A "Personal Qualities" section in your resumé that simply mirrors these skill areas isn't enough. To say that you have highly developed team-building skills, for example, doesn't mean that recruiters will automatically swoon at the very thought of you coming in to interview. No, they will expect to see a piece of evidence to back up your assertion. If you can show specifically how you demonstrated team-building qualities, then you might be in. Perhaps you might go for something along the following lines:

"It ain't what you do, it's the way that you do it.
That's what gets results."
As sung by ELLA FITZGERALD, BANANARAMA, and many more

Defining
idea…

Instigated a series of "Working in Harmony" workshops at a time when cross-team working was virtually nonexistent and morale generally low. Won the company's Team of the Year award, and the latest employee survey revealed a significant hike in morale levels.

With application forms, the challenge to provide evidence of various competencies is often made explicitly. Forms are often designed to include a series of headings like "Decision Making," "Leadership," and "Problem Solving." The applicant then has to give concrete examples of a time when they had to display effective decision-making skills, and so on.

Giving examples can be more difficult than you might imagine. How easy would you find it, say, to come up with an account of a time when you had to display a high level of integrity? It's not how most of us naturally file our organizational experience. Instead, we move from task to task, rarely pausing long enough to capture behavioral evidence from our work life. This becomes a real problem when we want to change jobs and we're asked to come up with lots of evidence and examples.

Q **Good grief! Has the world gone crazy? Competency systems seem like a new cottage industry for the HR department to me.**

How did it go?

A *That's not really true. Competency-based selection methods have actually been shown to be about the fairest recruitment system around. A competency-based approach is only concerned with what people actually do in their jobs; it's not concerned with job titles and it takes no note of how we might respond to hypothetical situations. Imagine you're in an interview and somebody asks you how you'd react in a crisis. In that hypothetical world, I'm sure that we'd all stay calm and show any necessary leadership traits. In the real world of competencies, the question would be along the lines of, "Tell me about a time when you've had to deal with a crisis situation." In response, we'd have to describe how we have actually behaved.*

Q **Enough! This is beginning to sound like a Competency Party broadcast. I'm not sure how to use competencies in my resumé, so can you concentrate on that, please?**

A *As I mentioned earlier, competencies are skills or characteristic actions we use to deal with situations in and outside of work. So, when you describe specifically how you did something, you're using competency language. This shows up in resumés in the form of action statements, i.e., what we actually did to achieve certain results. If you want to develop your fluency in "behaviorese," look at the list of competencies previously listed and see if you can come up with an example of a time when you needed to demonstrate each of those traits. Make a note of what you personally did and you have the makings of your own personal database.*

6

Reading the runes

How to interpret job postings and ensure your resumé reflects what's required.

OK, so you've scoured the papers, trade magazines, and the Web and you've come across something you rather like the sound of. Now comes the difficult part...

HOW TO ANALYZE AN ADVERTISEMENT

In their book *Brilliant CV*, British authors Jim Bright and Joanne Earl offer up a helpful set of questions that might enable you to get a grip on a job posting:

1. What don't you understand about the job ad?

2. What type of industry is it in? What's happening in the company or industry? Is it restructuring or expanding?

3. What is the main purpose of the role being offered?

4. Why is this role important to the company? How will this role affect the company's bottom line?

Here's an idea for you... **Be explicit about how you meet the specification in your cover letter. If the advertisement asks for somebody who can do A, B, and C, then your cover letter should detail how A, B, and C are the very things you do best.**

5. What type of skills do they want? What other skills might be needed, given the job's purpose?

6. What types of knowledge/training do they want? What other knowledge or training might be needed, given the job's purpose?

MATCHING REQUIREMENTS

Read the posting carefully to build up your diagnosis of the sort of person the recruiter is after. Differentiate between the essential requirements and those that are desirable. Most requirements will be explicit, but some may be implicit and require you to read between the lines.

For example, in March 2001 a town council was seeking applicants for a PR post that would involve promoting bus transportation, yet a company car was being offered with the job. A representative for the council was quoted as hoping that the person appointed would demonstrate personal commitment to the job by not taking the car offer. Now there's one way to impress/not impress the council!

Sometimes, what we imagine to be essential is sometimes either desirable or unnecessary. In July 2004, the British press reported with great amusement that the newly appointed chairman of the Melton Mowbray Pork Pie Association, Matthew O'Callaghan, was a vegetarian.

If the ad mentions a website reference, that's your first port of call research-wise. If it doesn't, it's still worth using a search engine to try to track down their website. A company's website will help you to build your understanding of the company and may well provide further information about the vacancy.

For more on figuring out if a job is right for you, turn to IDEA 7, *What am I getting myself into?*

Try another idea...

Ordinarily, you'll need to show that you can meet practically 100 percent of the essential requirements and around 50–70 percent of the desirable qualities sought. However, when the labor market is tight and there just aren't that many people job-hunting, you can afford to drop the former to 70–80 percent. The desirables become almost irrelevant if the recruiter is likely to get a low response to their advertisement.

When you examine the job requirements in detail, you'll find that you match each of the recruiter's requirements at different levels. These can be characterized as:

- High match
- Medium match
- Low or no match

Where you have a high match, make sure that this is glaringly apparent in both your cover letter and resumé. Where you have a medium match, include this in the resumé but not in the cover letter. If you can only muster a low match or no match, bury this toward the back of the resumé or, better still, don't mention it at all!

"Your insight serves you well."
OBI-WAN KENOBI

Defining idea...

How did it go?

Q **I've just seen a job that I'd love to apply for. What should I do next?**

A *Start by reading the job posting very carefully, asking yourself what the organization is looking for. Most of the requirements will be set out explicitly: experience of this; holding a qualification in that; proven leader/team-builder/decision-maker or whatever. Make a list of these requirements and ask yourself whether you meet them.*

Q **What if I don't have everything that the job posting asks for?**

A *It's often the case that applicants don't have every qualification or piece of experience mentioned in the listing. Try to determine what the "must-haves" are. These aren't necessarily what the ad describes as essential. For example, "Must have a good working knowledge of Sage accounting software" might in reality mean, "If you know a different piece of accounting software, we'd be prepared to pay for some Sage training to bring you up to speed." Also, "Must have a degree" often isn't as inflexible as it sounds. As a rough guideline, if you can match 70 percent of the stated requirements, it can be worth going for. After all, you've got nothing to lose but the price of a stamp. Oh and by the way, resist any miserly tendencies and go for first-class postage.*

7

What am I getting myself into?

The better you understand your target company, the more targeted you can make your resumé. Which is why you'd be wise to find out as much as possible about your next potential employer.

If you uncover a potential corporate "basket case," then I'd advise against joining them. If a company comes through your research with flying colors, however, then it should make an impressive addition to your resumé.

Here are five ways to carry out the research required to separate the Enrons of this world from the pick of the bunch:

1. Call a friend

Start putting the word around and you may track down somebody (or somebody who knows somebody) who either works for the company or is a customer or supplier of theirs. These informal sources of information can be an invaluable guide to what's really going on inside the company.

Here's an idea for you...

Ask yourself how good a potential employer is compared to where you're currently working. Remember that the company you go on to join will be the company that will take first place at the top of your resumé the next time you make a move. How do you think that will play with future employers? Will they be impressed?

2. Google them

The amount of information to be found on the Internet is quite staggering. In the pre-Internet days, it could be quite difficult to research a company. Nowadays, to show up at an interview without a detailed understanding of the company is almost unforgivable. You don't have to use Google, of course. Personally, I'm quite fond of www.mooter.com.

3. The company website

Most companies of any kind of size will have one. Many of the best sites include an online copy of annual reports, information on company structures, copies of vision or mission statements, press releases, and links to related sites. If you don't know the website address, it's always worth trying www.[name of company].com, .net, .info, etc. Failing that, a decent search engine should get you there pretty quickly. If there isn't a company website, that in itself carries a message.

Defining idea...

"To be conscious that you are ignorant is a great step to knowledge."
BENJAMIN DISRAELI

4. Get hold of an annual report

You can often do this online via the company's website. There are also a number of ordering services you can use. For example, it's worth using a service like AnnualReports.com, where you can ask for any number of reports to be

sent to your address free of charge.
Alternatively, call the companies directly and
ask them to send you a copy.

5. Track newspapers and journals
Scan the newspapers if you can, particularly the
broadsheets and business journals like the
Economist. If something is in the papers, chances are that the topic may well be high
in the minds of people who work there.

You should be able to directly incorporate some of the information you uncover
into your resumé or cover letter. In fact, this should be a specific aim of yours, as
there's real added value in letting the company know that you've put time and
effort into finding out about them. And, of course, should you be invited to
interview, you'll already have done a lot of the legwork to prepare yourself for that
part of the selection process.

One final point. Leaving one job for another is a
significant life decision. An informed decision is
always likely to yield a better outcome than a
leap into the dark. Before you think of
resigning, are you confident that you know
enough about the new role and the new
company, such as its culture, the state of the
balance sheet, and so on?

**If you're on the point of joining
another organization, consider
looking back at IDEA 1, *Dream
a little dream*, to make sure
you're still on track to achieve
your career goals.**

Try another idea...

**"I know all the tourist things.
I know about the Queen,
Buckingham Palace, driving
on the left-hand side of the
road, and fish and chips."**
MALACHI DAVIS, American athlete,
insisting he had the right
credentials to represent Great
Britain at the 2004 Olympics
(and did)

Defining idea...

How did it go?

Q **I've uncovered one or two pieces of information about a company I'm interested in that I'm not sure I like the looks of. What do I do now?**

A *This will depend on precisely what's concerning you. I'd suggest that you don't give even weight to every piece of information you dig up. If you've talked with somebody working inside the company and you're happy that they have given you a balanced view, then that probably deserves greater weight than some newspaper sources. If you've popped the company name into Google and have come across a website that features a rant by an ex-employee, be more sanguine. By and large, I recommend giving the company the benefit of the doubt. After all, if you don't apply for a job on the back of your research, you may never find out whether that research was unfair. You can always withdraw your application at a later stage.*

Q **I've come across a job I'd like to go for with a small start-up company, but unfortunately I'm really struggling to get any information at all about these people. How can I get the facts I need to make a decision?**

A *It's a fact of business life that some companies will have no track record to speak of, but perhaps they have marketing material they can send you or maybe even a business plan. I'd be a bit surprised at the lack of a website, but you may have no choice but to get into conversation with them and then make your judgment in light of what you have been able to discover.*

8

Numbers count

How to impress by numbers, using sales figures, savings, turnaround times, and other relevant metrics.

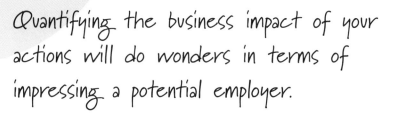

Quantifying the business impact of your actions will do wonders in terms of impressing a potential employer.

Did you know that the Charge of the Light Brigade, generally regarded as a catastrophic British military blunder, was actually nothing of the sort? According to Terry Brighton, author of a book about the battle, some 60 percent of the men who took part returned "without a scratch" and judged the encounter to be a success. I mention this not out of any revisionary zeal, but because I want to pick up on the phrase "some 60 percent of the men who took part." If instead of specifying "60 percent" the sentence stated "quite a few" or "the majority," would the sentence's meaning be conveyed as well? Let's face it, "60 percent" appears precise and unambiguous in a way that "quite a few" most certainly isn't.

Now I know that numbers shouldn't necessarily be taken at face value either. It's sometimes said that there are three types of lies: lies, damned lies, and statistics. Then of course there's that gibe that's often hurled at politicians, namely that they use statistics the way a drunk uses a lamppost—for support rather than illumination. However, these caveats aside, most people accept that numbers can carry a weight and conviction that mere words often struggle to emulate.

Here's an idea for you...

If you can't locate precise numbers to include in your resumé, then guesstimate. After all, if *you* can't find accurate data, it's unlikely that anybody from the organization you've applied to could prove you wrong.

AVOID AMBIGUITY

Use as much quantification as possible and you'll give your resumé genuine impact and authority. In contrast, there are words that can disguise a range of possible truths and these should be avoided at all costs. For example, what does it really mean when somebody writes that they "manage a small team"? Assuming we're not talking Snow White and the Seven Dwarfs here, the unvarnished truth could be "I manage thirty people," in which case you might be underselling yourself depending on how the reader interprets "small." Or it could be "I share one admin assistant with two other people," in which case the phrase "weasel words" comes to mind.

Another example is, "I introduced a more efficient system for managing overtime and achieved significant savings for the department." Does that mean that the applicant saved $250,000 a year or thirty bucks?

QUANTIFICATION IS THE NAME OF THE GAME

Opportunities to use quantification include:

- The number of people employed by the company
- Company turnover
- Division turnover
- Size of budgets you were responsible for
- Number of people managed
- Money you've saved the organization

- Improvements in turnaround times
- Improvements in productivity
- Improvements in levels of customer satisfaction
- Performance against sales targets
- Reduction in backlogs
- Achieving something against a tight timescale

You'll need to communicate these metrics with a bit of flair. More on this in IDEA 9, *Write with panache*.

Try another idea...

And here are four examples of quantified achievement statements:

1. Designed and successfully implemented a new set of shift rosters, reducing the department's wage bill by 12 percent.

   "Round numbers are always false."
   SAMUEL JOHNSON

   Defining idea...

2. Took over an ailing business and turned an annual loss of $8 million into a profit of $23 million within two years.

3. Exceeded sales target for the last financial year by 38 percent.

4. Increased the customer complaints dealt with within 24 hours from an average of 73 percent in 2003 to 98 percent in 2004.

Of course, in order to include some relevant metrics in your resumé you'll need to have access to the data. So, if you don't already have these numbers on hand, now's a good time to start rummaging through the departmental filing system.

"To measure is to know."
LORD BERKELEY, aristocrat and scientist

Defining idea...

How did it go?

Q **I've racked my brain and I'm struggling to come up with quantifiable information to put on my resumé. Now what?**

A *It's not always easy to quantify our impact in our role. Before giving up entirely though, ask yourself first why your job exists and second what the output is from your job. Answering the first question will clarify your broad purpose. Answering the second should provide a clue about metrics. If your role is to process claims, how many do you process in a given period? If you work in a shop, how many customers do you serve in a day and what are a typical day's takings? If you're a receptionist, how many people pass through your reception area? You may also find that the metrics in your work area don't operate at an individual level but rather at a team, departmental, or organizational level. Somewhere around you there will be numbers, I promise!*

Q **I've managed to come up with some numbers but frankly it's been a bad year for the company and they're not very impressive. Would I be better off keeping quiet?**

A *This problem often arises when trading conditions are difficult. It's easy enough to declare sales figures when they're up 18 percent on the previous year, but not so easy when they're down 18 percent. Even so, it can be worth putting your performance in context. If your numbers are down 18 percent against an industry average that's down 37 percent, then it's actually something to be proud of!*

Write with panache

Let's look at some ways to up your linguistic skills and make a great impression.

Putting together a top-notch resumé involves a balancing act between the conventions of resumé writing and the need to try to stand out from the competition.

Emperor Charles V is probably best known for his remark: "I speak Spanish to God, Italian to women, French to men, and German to my horse."

I repeat this remark not to upset my German readers, but to illustrate a core truth about the nature of effective communication: Getting your message across is about adapting your approach to the needs of your audience.

As a general principle, you're more likely to stand out for content than style. That said, a stylistically inept resumé will undermine even excellent content. And for that reason, it's important to observe the stylistic conventions of resumé writing. Here are five useful habits to adopt:

Here's an idea for you...

Use the latest buzzwords. Being unaware of everyday phrases in a particular industry will show a lack of research on your part. Make yourself familiar with the latest business jargon, for example "core competences" instead of skills. Avoid clichés like the plague!

Keep it snappy

You don't need to use complete sentences. Concise, understandable phrases are sufficient. No sentence fragments, however. They are very. Irritating. To read.

Loiter within tense

Aim to maintain a consistent approach to tense throughout. Most if not all of your resumé should be written in the past tense. After all, the light dust of history has settled on all of your previous jobs. When you're describing the role you're in now, some elements will be current, such as the work you do on a day-to-day basis. Other parts will be in the past, however, such as the project you led that finished a few months ago or maybe last quarter's results.

If you have a combination of present and past bullet-points to convey, cluster the present together and report them first. This may sound a bit finicky, but mixing them up just looks plain wrong.

Defining idea...

"Words, like Nature, half reveal And half conceal the Soul within."
LORD TENNYSON, "In Memoriam AHH"

Use the third person

Write about yourself in the third person rather than the first. This will lend an air of objectivity and professionalism to the proceedings that using "I," "me," and "my" lacks.

Avoid confusing turns of phrase

I once received a resumé from an applicant who claimed that he could "fire people with enthusiasm." He wasn't invited to interview and so I still don't know whether he meant that he was a superb motivator or that he could sack people with gusto. Check that you've expressed yourself as clearly as possible throughout. Even better, get someone else to read your resumé, as they'll spot things that would sail past you unchallenged.

Powerful language is important but IDEA 5, *Learn to speak "behaviorese,"* shows you still need to craft it into a format that'll have the highest impact.

Try another idea...

Don't try to be funny

You may have a take on life that's so amusing that your dinner party stories hospitalize accountants, but it's a different story when it comes to your resumé. Humor depends on knowing your audience; you don't know the person who'll be assessing your resumé so don't go there. And remember that puns are for children, not groan readers. (Sorry, couldn't resist it!)

Use plain English

In his 1946 essay "Politics and the English Language," George Orwell came up with a set of six rules for writing plainly and clearly. I think you'll agree they hold up very well as a set of principles for anybody writing their resumés today:

"The play was a great success but the audience was a disaster."
OSCAR WILDE

Defining idea...

1. Never use a metaphor, simile, or other figure of speech that you're used to seeing in print.

2. Never use a long word where a short one will do.

3. If it's possible to cut a word out, always cut it out.

4. Never use the passive voice where you can use the active.

5. Never use a foreign phrase, a scientific word, or a jargon word if you can think of an everyday English equivalent.

6. Break any of these rules sooner than say anything barbarous.

How did it go?

Q   **Look, I'm no J. K. Rowling. If I was, I wouldn't be working for Scroggins Engineering; I'd be whooping it up with the literati in Cuba, wouldn't I?**

A   *Point taken, but I'm not suggesting that having a successful corporate career depends on your gaining a Masters in Creative Writing. The techniques I'm talking about here come down to some straightforward, easy-to-follow guidelines.*

Q   **OK, I get the basic idea—consistent tense, third person, plain language, no jokes, and so on. Is that all there is to this?**

A   *Yes, but don't underestimate how difficult it is to write plainly and clearly. Quite often, we're our own worst judges when it comes to our writing. We think we've been the model of clarity and brevity, only to find out that somebody reading our output gets confused about what we mean. The acid test of our writing isn't whether we think it's good, it's what other people make of it. To that end, and I know this is a bit of a recurring theme, I'd always recommend showing your resumé and cover letter to a few people before you start sending it out.*

10

The seven deadly resumé sins

Sometimes success is about the things we do; sometimes it's more about the things we don't do...

The biggest resumé sin is probably to bore the pants off the reader, but there are plenty of other pitfalls awaiting the inattentive amongst us.

When we go in search of these pitfalls, do we find that the traditional seven deadly sins—Pride, Avarice, Envy, Wrath, Lust, Gluttony, and Sloth—hold any lessons for the modern-day resumé writer? Maybe, but some are admittedly more tenuous than others.

PRIDE

Pride can lead us to overstate our abilities. So, don't go describing your IT skills as "excellent" when you know little more than how to turn on your PC. Equally, don't enclose a photo because you're good-looking, unless you're a model, actor, or actress, of course.

Avoid unnecessary repetition in your resumé. Do not repeat things. Say them only once. Do not say them twice. Or three times. Once is enough. (Now can you see how irritating repetition is?)

AVARICE

Avarice can lead us to apply for jobs that are well beyond our capabilities. In truth, we're often more attracted to the salary than to the job itself.

The opposite of avarice is generosity. This means letting others have their fair share of praise. Don't claim personal credit for a team achievement. Acknowledging the contributions of others from time to time will demonstrate that you can be a team player. On the other hand, don't "we" all over your resumé or else you'll have the recruiter struggling to detect what you specifically bring to the party.

ENVY

Envy is about resenting the good others receive or the qualities they possess. In the context of resumé writing, envy might come out in the form of sniping at the effort of others, which is a dangerous tactic. As a Russian proverb puts it, "He who digs a hole for another may fall in it himself."

"Men are liars. We'll lie about lying if we have to. I'm an algebra liar. I figure two good lies make a positive."
TIM ALLEN, actor

Alternatively, we might feel tempted to claim experience and qualifications we don't possess in order to appear on an equal footing with others.

WRATH

Wrath is a furious level of anger that we'd like to vent on someone or something. If we've left or are leaving our current organization on less than harmonious terms, maybe on the back of an acrimonious layoff, there's a very human tendency to want to express those feelings. Just remember that your resumé isn't the right place for this. It must remain a professional, dispassionate document—anything more emotive will do you more harm than good.

For some hints on giving an honest resumé some sparkle, take a look at IDEA 9, *Write with panache*.

Try another idea…

LUST

Lust is the self-destructive drive for pleasure out of proportion to its worth. Lust causes us to suspend rational judgment in the pursuit of gratification.

Remember that you're not obliged to accept the first job offer that comes your way. The offer may be flattering, but feel free to turn it down if it's a poor fit for the criteria you've set for your ideal job—salary level, degree of challenge in the role, location, future prospects, and so on. On the other hand, when an offer meets most, but not all, of your criteria, you may choose to accept it or see if you can improve on the offer through discussion.

"If you tell the truth you don't have to remember anything."
MARK TWAIN

Defining idea…

"Some rise by sin, and some by virtue fall."
WILLIAM SHAKESPEARE

GLUTTONY

An overindulgent resumé gives too much detail and goes on for too many pages.

An opposite of gluttony is moderation. The perfect resumé gives the reader the right amount of information. Not too little to prevent the reader from really understanding what you have to offer. Equally not so much information that the reader is swamped with unnecessary detail.

SLOTH

Sloth is about an inclination to be lazy and to put in little effort. With resumé writing, there are two areas where lack of effort will undermine success. The first is where we simply take our old resumé and bring it up to date rather than going for a radical overhaul and rewrite. The second is where we don't put enough effort into adapting our resumé for each job we apply for.

Q **I recently read a book called *Sin to Win*. Are you telling me sinning is back in the doghouse?**

How did it go?

A *In this case, yes. This idea is simply intended to reinforce the point that sometimes best practice is about the things we should do and sometimes about the things we shouldn't.*

Q **Is this a definitive list of sins?**

A *Absolutely not, but it's a reminder that some things definitely don't work well in your resumé. Speaking of which, in August 2004 a recruitment firm called Marketing Professionals came up with its own list of the top ten resumé sins, namely:*

■ *Typos—around 50 percent of resumés contain spelling mistakes or grammatical errors.*

■ *Work experience listed in the wrong order—recruiters recommend you put the most recent position first.*

■ *Unexplained gaps in dates between jobs—if you've taken time off, you should say why.*

■ *Sloppy formatting—using inappropriate fonts, mixing up styles and sizes, failing to align paragraphs or bullet points, etc.*

How did it go?

■ Trying to brighten things up with inappropriate use of colors, photographs, logos, or fancy paper—this rarely puts you at the top of the pile.

■ Including irrelevant information such as holiday jobs or casual work.

■ Sending a resumé that has been constructed to apply for a different role—employers prefer one tailored to their vacancy.

■ A disorganized and hard-to-follow resumé, with information scattered around the page.

■ Too much information—resumés should be kept to one or two pages and long paragraphs and sentences should be avoided.

■ Too little information—if it's too basic it won't interest the employer.

11

Looks can kill

Content is obviously important but so is presentation, so take the time to get it right.

If your resumé is poorly presented, chances are that nobody will bother to read it. Here are some tips on how to present your resumé both professionally and attractively.

Don't let this go any further, but I've reached the age where catching a glimpse of myself in a mirror first thing in the morning isn't a cheery experience. It's as though makeup artists from *The Lord of the Rings* wait until I fall asleep and spend the night producing a look that might be characterized as "Orc with an attitude problem." The fact is, these days Middleton *au naturel* is a babe magnet to whom the iron filings of sexual attraction show a studied indifference. On the other hand, give me the time to doll myself up and I can walk freely in public places without scaring all but the most sensitive of souls.

You can probably see where this is leading in the context of high-impact resumés. Elsewhere in this book we've looked at the importance of getting the language and tone of the resumé right. But it's just as important for the look and layout to be easy on the reader's eye.

Here's an idea for you... **Choose just one font that's clear, distinct, and easy to read, such as Arial, Times Roman, Verdana, or Gill Sans. Using lots of different fonts will look messy.**

THE KEY TO A GOOD-LOOKING RESUMÉ

1. Your resumé should be typed, of course. A handwritten version might show you're a quirky individualist, but most recruiters will regard you as somebody who either can't use or can't be bothered to gain access to a computer. Neither of these will endear a candidate to a company.

2. Use quality paper, typically white, which photocopies the best. There are those who swear by using tinted paper in the belief that this helps their resumé catch the eye. Most recruiters, however, swear with equal force that this doesn't make a blind bit of difference. Whatever you do, don't go down the fluorescent pink route—it looks ugly and it's as though the paper is impregnated with a whiff of desperation.

3. Avoid front covers and fancy bindings. A recruiter wants to read your resumé, not unwrap it! Pretentious packaging will almost certainly condemn your resumé to the reject pile.

Defining idea... *"She got her good looks from her father. He's a plastic surgeon."*
GROUCHO MARX

4. Don't send out poor-quality photocopies of your resumé, as this will give the impression that you're mailing your resumé en masse and don't care who employs you.

5. Keep the content uncluttered. Edit it so that every line adds value. By ruthlessly excising extraneous information, you give yourself the opportunity to wrap lots of white space around the text. This looks good and is very handy for the recruiter to make notes on.

Still tempted to go for something a bit more flamboyant? IDEA 17, *Set the right tone*, should dispel any such career-damaging thoughts.

Try another idea...

6. Use bullet points, bold type, spacing, etc., to make the resumé look as attractive and readable as possible. That said, don't ever just have a single bullet point, as this will look sloppy and inattentive.

7. Unless your resumé is sponsored by LensCrafters, keep your font size at around the 11 or 12 point mark. I've seen so many resumés where the writer has reduced the font size in order to cram as much information as possible into two pieces of paper. It's not a pretty sight and predisposes the reader to earmark you for a "no thanks" letter.

8. Watch out for typos and grammatical areas. Perhaps I'm old-fashioned, but my response to the person who scrawled "You loosers" (sic) on the wall at Fenway Park, in response to the team's defeat, was to castigate their spelling ability rather than applaud the sentiment expressed.

"People don't bat an eyelid about using moisturizers."
JONNY WILKINSON, on life in the England rugby team's locker room, which demonstrates that appearance counts in the most unlikely settings

Defining idea...

How did it go?

Q **I've just put together my resumé, incorporating some of this advice. I know that presentation is important but is all this really necessary?**

A *When I cover this topic at resumé-writing workshops, there's invariably one person who balks at the idea that style is as important as substance, arguing that surely excellent content is the key thing to get right. They have a bit of a point—immaculately presented dross is unlikely to gain you an interview, whereas poorly presented but substantial content just might. It's a false argument though. Far and away your best chance of securing an interview is for your resumé to be both substantial and attractively presented.*

Q **OK, I'm prepared to be convinced that appearance makes a difference. What's the biggest blunder that we can make in presentation?**

A *In my view, just about the biggest blunder is somebody sending their resumé out using their current employer's stationery and fax machine. Being regarded as somebody who steals office supplies is not the best recommendation to a new employer. In fact, I know recruiters who take such umbrage at that practice that, as soon as they realize what has happened, they trash or shred the envelope and contents.*

54

12

Two resumés are better than one

Inside information on how to produce a tailor-made resumé for each application.

Applying for jobs was different back in the 1980s. I remember one job-hunting phase where I sat at home listening to Frankie Goes to Hollywood while scouring the papers and cutting out any appealing job ads.

Every time I found one, I'd take a resumé from my pile of photocopies, pop it in an envelope, address the envelope, add a stamp, and voilà—application to go. I used to time myself doing this; my unratified record was thirty-seven seconds.

To be fair, that particular approach was partly a product of the technology available back then. Changing your resumé was a bit of a palaver, which typically involved gaining access to somebody with a manual typewriter or (if you were lucky) an early word processor the size of a refrigerator and trying to charm them into spending an hour of their time helping you produce a new version.

Locate a couple of advertisements—one for the type of role you're currently filling and one in a new field that you'd be interested in. Put together a tailored version of your resumé for each role, making sure that you highlight the key attributes you have to offer in each case.

These days, of course, pretty much everybody has access to a PC—almost certainly at work and probably at home—and so revising our resumés ought not to be beyond our wit and technological powers. This is just as well because just as the world has moved on since the 1980s (not to mention my musical taste) employers' expectations about the quality of resumés have risen sharply.

Nowadays, a resumé isn't simply a statement of career experience to date, but a marketing document. And not just an ordinary marketing document either, but a *one-to-one* marketing document. What this means is that your resumé needs to be customized to each and every job you apply for. To put it bluntly, if you're not producing a customized document every time your resumé goes out, you're significantly reducing the likelihood of getting an interview.

Two key questions you need to ask yourself every time you put pen to paper are:

"The highest importance in the art of detection is to be able to recognize out of a number of facts which are incidental and which are vital."
SHERLOCK HOLMES

1. What does the organization with the vacancy want?

2. What do I have to offer that matches what the organization is looking for?

To take each in turn:

WHAT DOES THE ORGANIZATION WITH THE VACANCY WANT?

This is fairly straightforward when the vacancy is advertised because all the information you need should be in the advertisement or contained in an information pack that the organization will send you if you express an interest.

Where you've heard of the vacancy through the grapevine and there isn't a formal job posting as such, you can still make an intelligent guess at the qualities required. If you can back that up with a talk with somebody who might give you some inside information on the vacancy, so much the better. Best of all, call the manager with the vacancy directly to establish what they're after.

WHAT DO I HAVE TO OFFER THAT MATCHES WHAT THE ORGANIZATION IS LOOKING FOR?

Show specifically how your experience matches the company's needs. If its job posting asks for someone who's worked with younger staff and you've had experience introducing three trainees into the department who've all gone on to be offered permanent positions, make sure you convey this.

If you've been able to speak to the manager with the vacancy, make sure that you've incorporated how you'd be able to meet their stated needs.

To delve more deeply into the art of interpreting job advertisements, turn to IDEA 6, *Reading the runes.*

Try another idea...

How did it go?

Q **I'm really struggling with this "one-to-one marketing document" concept. Are you telling me there's no place for old-school resumés?**

A *As far as I'm concerned, the old-school resumé has gone the way of the DeLorean and Betamax. If you have no idea what I'm talking about, then I think I've made my point! If you do remember, then you've been around long enough to know that life moves on. New technologies make new things possible. These days, most of us have ready access to a PC and Internet connection. As a result, it's never been easier to create, update, and store documents. Plus, quality research into companies is now only a search engine away. As soon as a few people realized they could outpace the competition by producing specific resumés for specific jobs, job hunting entered a new era.*

Q **All right, I accept that standards have risen, but surely when the job market is tight and there are fewer people looking to change jobs, employers can't afford to be too picky, can they?**

A *You're right to say that a tight job market typically means fewer applicants. There's no real evidence, however, that employers have to drop their standards. If there are only ten applicants but nine resumés are better than yours, you're likely to end up on the "reserve" pile at best.*

13

How to deal with the skeletons in your resumé

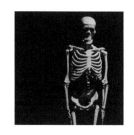

Want to know how to fix the gaps in your resumé or a track record that would qualify you for membership in Job-Hoppers Anonymous?

In an ideal world, we'd all have unimpeachable working histories and picture-perfect resumés. In reality, we may have a skeleton (or at least a metatarsal) or two in the career closet.

Here are two slightly tricky career scenarios that you may have to deal with:

GAPS

The year you took off to write your as yet unpublished novel, the six months you spent bumming around the world, or that decade when you just didn't feel like working—many of us have acquired gaps in our career history. Although there's a tendency to assume that employers will see these gaps as negative, that's not always the case.

Review your job history and go over any elements that you aren't currently comfortable talking about. Any discomfort on your part will be picked up by a professional interviewer, so develop a story line that you feel comfortable with.

The absolute golden rule is not to leave a gap in your resumé unaccounted for. Recruiters who notice gaps such as these are likely to think the applicant is less honest than average. On the other hand, if recruiters notice a gap for which an explanation is provided, then the applicant is typically thought to be more honest than average.

There's also some evidence to show that it's possible to turn gaps between jobs to your advantage. The trick is to be very positive about both what you did and what you got out of it. If you're able to identify job-relevant skills that you picked up along the way, then you have no worries.

JOB-HOPPING

Let's say that you have a career history that would have qualified you for Job-hopper of the Year several years running. For temporary positions, this normally won't be a problem because you'll simply be maintaining an already established pattern. If you're applying for a permanent job, however, there are things you can do to make the most of your colorful past so that you're not seen as a corporate commitment-phobe.

Defining idea...

"Don't be afraid to give your best to what seemingly are small jobs. Every time you conquer one it makes you that much stronger. If you do the little jobs well, the big ones tend to take care of themselves."
DALE CARNEGIE

The key to success is to present your career using a functional resumé format. This type of resumé, as you may remember from earlier, focuses on skills and achievements, in contrast to the reverse chronological model that emphasizes each individual role you've held.

If you're still concerned about making a negative impression, try IDEA 21, Detox your resumé.

Try another idea...

Using a functional approach, you can devote the first page of your resumé to drawing relevant information from across the full range of jobs you've held. Place this evidence under headings that are relevant to the vacancy you're applying for, such as decision-making, handling customers, team working, etc. Employers will expect to see a job history somewhere on your resumé, but by putting it on page two you'll be downplaying its significance a bit.

REMEMBER ABRAHAM LINCOLN

You may find that some employers will decline the opportunity to give you a job despite your very best presentational efforts. Risk-averse organizations whose natural preference is for stolid, dull, unadventurous recruits may find your past just a bit too colorful. Then again, would you really want a job in those types of place?

It's worth remembering that persistence will pay off as long as you keep throwing your resumé hat into the employment ring. Not only will it pay off, but it may yield spectacularly

"Whatever you are, be a good one."
ABRAHAM LINCOLN

Defining idea...

good results over the long term. Abraham Lincoln had many a setback in his life and career as the following record shows:

1832   Defeated in the race for the legislature
1833   Failed in business
1834   Elected to legislature
1835   Sweetheart died
1836   Suffered a nervous breakdown
1838   Defeated for speaker in the legislature
1843   Defeated for nomination to Congress
1846   Elected to Congress
1848   Lost renomination
1849   Rejected for job as land officer
1854   Defeated for Senate
1856   Defeated for nomination for vice-president
1858   Defeated for Senate
1860   Elected sixteenth president of the United States

So, take comfort from Abe's resumé and don't ever give up.

Q **I've had many jobs over the past five years, but now I've decided I want to take my career a bit more seriously and find some long-term employment. What's the best way to present my errant past?**

How did it go?

A *Don't present a comprehensive list showing how you spent two months here or three months there. Instead, consider rolling them all up under one heading along the lines of: "1999–2004: Various temporary positions." In order to convince an employer that you're now a safe recruitment bet you'll need to explain why you held so many temporary jobs and why you haven't sought a permanent position until now. For example: "During this period, I was a member of a semi-professional band that regularly toured the US, making it impractical to take on a permanent position. The band split up in late 2003."*

Q **That's helpful. Are there any other strategies I could use?**

A *You may also find that you can cluster jobs into related groups. For example, if you worked in eight restaurants over a two-year period, rather than list the individual restaurants and the periods you spent at each one, you could soften things by writing it up along the following lines: "1999–2001: Various front of house positions in clubs and restaurants. During this period, I took a number of temporary jobs working in places like McDonald's, T.G.I. Fridays, and Outback Steak House. These jobs helped me to develop a high level of confidence in dealing with customers, sometimes in situations that required high levels of tact and diplomacy."*

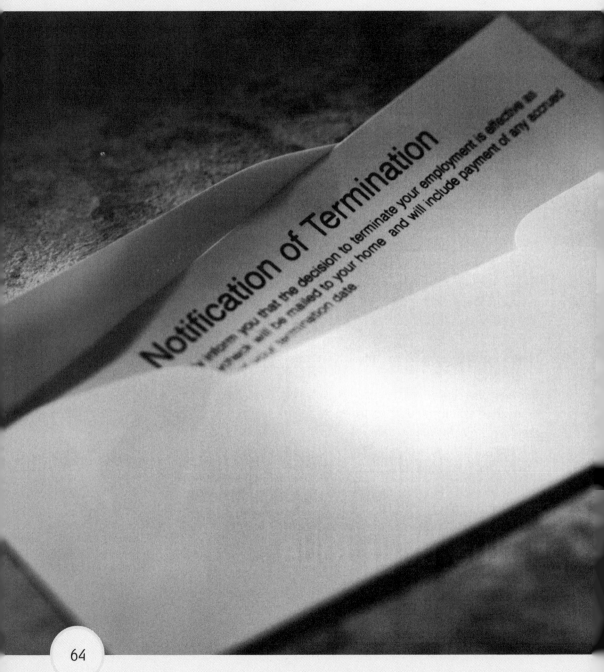

14

Another skeleton, another closet: layoffs

Being laid off isn't the showstopper it once was, but you still need to be careful how you convey this news to an interviewer.

Being laid off used to be an unmentionable topic. These days we're more accustomed to it, but there are still at least two lingering myths about its significance.

MYTH 1: THEY BROUGHT IT ON THEMSELVES

Back in the strife-ridden 1970s, some companies would use layoffs as an opportunity to give troublemakers, ne'er-do-wells, and social misfits the ax. Consequently, anyone laid off found themselves regarded with some suspicion by the job market, even when the real problem was more likely to be incompetent management that left companies in financial doo-doo.

Here's an idea for you... **When explaining the background to your layoff, avoid any hint of negativity and never contemplate using the phrase "personality clash" as that'll give the recruiter the willies and ensure you don't make the short list. Try rehearsing your answer. Why not test it out on a sympathetic ear?**

Not anymore. Layoffs have become commonplace. The vast majority of layoffs come on the back of a downturn in business, restructuring within a business, or mergers. Against this backdrop, most people who are laid off are simply in the wrong role at the wrong time.

MYTH 2: IT'S EASIER TO GET A JOB FROM A JOB

Job seekers seem to think that employers are better disposed to applicants with jobs and that applicants are at a disadvantage if they're on the market due to layoffs. Again, not true. Statistically there's no evidence to back this up.

These days, most recruiters pay little heed to layoffs when assessing the suitability of a candidate. In fact, quite a few recruiters regard it as a positive because it means that the individual is definitely in play, as opposed to applying for other jobs as a means of leveraging a better deal back at the ranch. It also means that the applicant is likely to be available at short notice.

HERE'S THE DEAL

There really isn't any stigma attached to being laid off anymore, as long as you effectively manage how you pass on this news. The key is to come up with an explanation in your cover letter that makes you sound professional and positive about losing your job.

Is there any merit in keeping quiet? I don't think so and here's one reason why:

Imagine you've applied for a job and been invited to an interview. Up comes the inevitable question, "Why are you looking to move on from your current role?" You explain that you've been laid off. A look of surprise is followed by a puzzled frown from the interviewer, who scans your resumé and cover letter to see if they missed something. This isn't good news because the interviewer now has a sense that you haven't been entirely open in your resumé, which will lead them to speculate what else you haven't disclosed.

So, my unambiguous advice is to come clean, presenting the most positive spin that you can. Here's one example of how you might convey the news in your letter: "Following a restructuring of the business, the entire New York division was closed down and I was one of thirty people affected. I was offered a role elsewhere in the company, but have decided that the time is right to seek out a role in a company that can offer me…"

You'll have your own variation of the facts, of course. Just make sure that you demonstrate your stoic quality.

Now start thinking about the bigger picture by turning to IDEA 23, *Managing the brand called You.*

Try another idea…

"It's a recession when your neighbor loses his job; it's a depression when you lose your own."
HARRY S TRUMAN

Defining idea…

"Always bear in mind that your own resolution to succeed is more important than any other one thing."
ABRAHAM LINCOLN

Defining idea…

How did it go?

Q **I'm surprised you say that most recruiters pay little heed to layoffs. I've been advised that I shouldn't mention the "L" word until I'm being interviewed. Is this incorrect?**

A *It's true that a few career advisers still act as though there's something vaguely shameful about being let go. According to their view of the job market, if you're unemployed or have been laid off, you shouldn't mention it in your initial approach for fear it might discourage a potential employer. In my opinion, that's total nonsense. For the past seven years, I've worked with people who've been laid off and I've yet to come across a case where it looked like declaring the layoff in the resumé or cover letter did any harm. And I know plenty of recruiters who are adamant that they'd prefer to know and that it's not regarded as a detrimental factor.*

Q **Now that I've been laid off, is there anything else I should be doing?**

A *If you can secure some outplacement support as part of your leaving package, grab it. It will be particularly helpful if it's been a few years since you were last active in the external job market. There are some excellent providers in the outplacement market who'll help you think through what needs to go into your resumé, critique your early drafts, give you some interview practice, and generally help you tune up for the marketplace.*

15

Selling a one-company career

It is possible to convey a one-company career to your advantage without suggesting that you're boring or lacking in ambition (even if you are).

After all, it wasn't that far back in the corporate time line when change used to happen in bursts, if at all.

Occasionally, a new CEO would turn up on the doorstep, have a rush of blood to the head, and personally redesign the business on the back of attending an executive seminar. Senior managers would sigh, brace themselves for a few bumpy months, and look forward to a time when life in the company would settle down again.

Then, in the mid- to late 1980s, companies realized they'd have to flick the change switch to on, and things have never been the same since. These days, constant change is an unquestioned given on most corporate agendas.

Here's an idea for you...

Find some positive adjectives to describe yourself. You have every right to play up the fact that you're "committed," "professional," "experienced," and a "team contributor."

What's all this got to do with how to present a one-company career in your resumé? Quite simply this: It used to be the case that in terms of experience a twenty-five-year stint with one organization was likely to amount to one year lived twenty-five times over. When the pace of change was low, there was little need for organizations to substantially change their operating patterns and as a result roles in the company tended to be about delivering a consistent performance year in and out. Staff turnover stayed fairly low and opportunities for personal growth and development were limited for many.

Over the last fifteen to twenty years, that situation has changed markedly. Driven by factors like global competition and developments in information technology, companies now expect a much higher level of flexibility and adaptability from their staff.

It has admittedly become less common for people to spend such long periods with one company, but those who do choose to stay (or just forget to leave) do have a plausible and convincing story line to present to potential employers.

The key is to assemble your resumé in such a way that it shows good progression within the company and a track record of acquiring new skills. In terms of presentation, put the most emphasis on what you've been doing over the last four to six years. And if you've had more than six roles in the company, don't list every single role and describe key responsibilities for each. The roles that you filled in the

1970s and 80s are unlikely to score many brownie points with the typical twenty-first-century recruiter. Instead, you might do well to wrap up that period into a catch-all couple of sentences. Possibly something along the lines of: "Early Career: Shortly after joining Scroggins Engineering in 19XX as a junior accounts clerk, I was transferred onto the junior management development program. I went on to achieve a number of promotions before being appointed to the role of Finance Manager in 19XX."

Quantify your achievements to demonstrate the impact you've had in your organization. For more on this see IDEA 8, *Numbers count.*

Try another idea...

OK, time for a quick reality check. There will be companies that won't take your application seriously simply because of your high level of corporate fidelity. If they're convinced that they want a young, ambitious, and dynamic person, they might well think that they're unlikely to detect those qualities in a career trajectory that shows solid and steady progression over a number of years. Bizarrely, this has little to do with an applicant's actual qualities and more to do with unshiftable stereotypes.

Generally though, if you set about describing your career positively, emphasizing everything you've achieved, there's no reason why your resumé should pale in comparison with any of the job-hopping competition.

"Individual commitment to a group effort—that is what makes a team work, a company work, a society work, a civilization work."
VINCE LOMBARDI, football coach

Defining idea...

71

Q **I've applied for several jobs that I felt I was very qualified for, but I haven't had a single interview. Am I doing something wrong?**

A *Not necessarily. It may just be the state of the market. That said, it's always possible that your resumé is letting you down. The most important thing is to focus on what you've been doing over the last four to six years. Don't give equal weight to all your jobs—this is a resumé, not an attempt to set out a balanced and proportionate picture of your life to date. The fact that you held a particular role for ten years back in the 1980s and early 1990s doesn't merit the role getting more than three or four lines at the most, even if it was the best job you ever had. It may have been a good time for you, but it's past it sell-by date in the resumé world.*

Q **Anything else I should watch out for?**

A *Watch out for any elements that counter any suggestion that you're a dried-out organizational husk. Make your resumé achievement-oriented; use positive, enthusiastic language; and include a profile statement to give your resumé a more contemporary look.*

16

My hobbies are Ping-Pong, playing the ukulele, and going to the theater

Do personal interests impress recruiters? They can, particularly if you think carefully about the mix you choose to outline.

The vast majority of recruiters and career advisers are pretty much in agreement about what constitutes a good resumé: comprehensive contact details, a profile statement, lots of examples of personal impact, reverse chronology, typically no more than two pages, keywords, and no jargon or acronyms.

Here's an idea for you... **As an alternative to a separate section on your personal hobbies and interests, consider going for a section called, say, "Other Information" and include hobbies and interests alongside things like your skills.**

Funnily enough, the area that seems to divide opinions most is the seemingly innocuous personal hobbies and interests section. The crucial question is whether including details of personal leisure activities and interests is liable to boost or reduce the impact of a resumé.

In one corner are those recruiters who believe that a section on personal interests gives resumé writers an opportunity to provide a more rounded version of themselves. They see it as our chance to show that there's more to us than merely being a corporate workhorse.

In the other corner, you'll find those who think that any suggestion of a life beyond work is at best a distraction and at worst a strong reason for the recruiting organization to doubt whether they'd get their pound of flesh. After all, somebody who, for example, spends their weekends and evenings pursuing a sport and who also serves on the parents' association of their children's school may not automatically be at the beck and call of their employer.

In my opinion, and I have to stress it is only an opinion (I've not been able to track down any reliable research to conclusively point one way or the other), I'd recommend that you do include some personal interest information. I've worked in two blue-chip companies in recruitment roles and have handled a lot of recruitment assignments and I've never come across a situation where a candidate who sets out their personal interests has suffered as a result. (I suppose theoretically if you mentioned that you did a lot of fundraising for a research laboratory that boasted the world's largest number of smoking beagles, then your application to be director of an animal rights organization may find itself on shaky ground. But it stretches the credulity that anybody would be foolish enough to include an interest that suggests a lack of empathy with the goals and aims of the organization they've applied to.)

Your interests are a component of your personal brand. You can find more on how to cultivate this in IDEA 23, *Manage the brand called You.*

Try another idea...

On the other hand, I've witnessed several instances where an applicant has mentioned a hobby or interest that coincidentally is shared by the person recruiting and where that common interest is enough to shift the applicant's resumé from the "not sure" pile to the "to be interviewed" pile.

The secret when describing your interests is not to go overboard. Mention a dozen outside interests and the recruiting company might legitimately wonder whether you'd have the energy to show up at work each day. Mention three or four and you suggest that you're a rounded individual.

Within those three or four, you should try to give an example of each of the following:

1. A mental activity—to show that you have brains to go with brawn.

2. A team-based or cooperative activity—to show that you're not some kind of bunny-boiling psycho-loner and that you can mix with other people.

"Develop interest in life as you see it; in people, things, literature, music—the world is so rich, simply throbbing with rich treasures, beautiful souls, and interesting people."
HENRY MILLER

Defining idea...

How did
it go?

Q   **I can't stand the thought of revealing personal information to a complete stranger. Isn't this information irrelevant in terms of my ability to do the job?**

A   *Technically. Unless there are specific allowed criteria for the advertised job, you don't have to include personal details such as your date of birth, sex, nationality, interests, marital status, or whether or not you have children. The key issue, however, isn't so much whether or not you choose to provide this sort of data, but more whether recruiters are likely to be ill-disposed to candidates who choose not to. Since the basis on which we're selected for an interview or rejected is shrouded in as much mystery as a papal election, it's very hard to get ahold of solid information in this respect.*

Q   **So, should I keep my personal data to myself or not?**

A   *Personally, I tend to be a pragmatist in this terrain and provide most personal data. I suppose I'm hitting a point in my life where age discrimination might rear its wrinkled head, but I figure that any recruiter worth their salt should be able to figure out my age to within a year or two from the information given in my resumé such as schooling details. Besides, most personal data isn't really that personal. It's not like employers want details of our bowel movements or how often we have sex.*

17

Set the right tone

OK, so you want to get noticed but you also want that interview, so don't go over the top in terms of wackiness. Here's what you need to know...

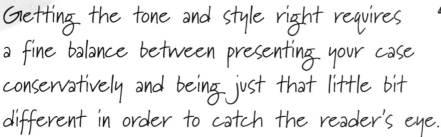
Getting the tone and style right requires a fine balance between presenting your case conservatively and being just that little bit different in order to catch the reader's eye.

The job marketplace has an overwhelmingly conservative outlook. You may come across the occasional recruitment consultant whose palate is jaded through seeing too many resumés and who will advise you that doing something radically different with yours is an important way of distinguishing yourself from the pack. But for every iconoclast like that, you'll find a hundred other recruitment consultants who will tell you that playing it safe is the best strategy.

This is not terribly exciting advice, but for the vast majority of jobs it's counterproductive to do anything more radical that substituting two sheets of white paper with two sheets of cream paper. To do anything more extreme is simply to create "noise" around your resumé that's more likely to distract than attract.

Here's an idea for you...

Unleash your creative streak and put together a resumé that has as many wacky features as you can stomach. Then compare it with your "normal" resumé. Which version would you honestly prefer to have circulating in the job marketplace? Can you draw anything at all from the wacky version that would improve the positive impact of your usual version?

So, here are a few dos and don'ts in terms of how to present your resumé to the job market:

DON'T send a photo

What is enclosing a photograph intended to achieve anyway? That you're young and virile and have your own head of hair? That your brow is furrowed with the wisdom of years? That you have a sharp dress sense? No, the fact is that recruiters don't like photos and in these politically correct times it's not palatable to imply that how you look should have some kind of bearing on whether or not you're interviewed.

DON'T use humor

There are few better ways of bonding with somebody than through a shared joke. But be warned. It's one thing to crack a funny in a convivial setting with a bunch of friends when the drink has been flowing freely; it's another thing entirely to insert something "amusing" into your resumé and then for your resumé to turn up under the nose of a complete stranger who may be having a rotten day and who may not share your sense of humor. Don't risk it.

DON'T mess with people's expectations

Recruiters expect to see a resumé set out in a standard format using a sensible font. Any attempt on your part to subvert those expectations is more likely to rebound on you than anything else.

DO match the resumé to the job you're going for

Most job applications benefit from a fairly conservative approach. The only exceptions are for jobs where a talent for innovation or creativity is explicitly required by the jobholder. In those rare cases, trying something a little bolder or more outlandish might bring home the bacon.

DO dress conservatively

If your resumé secures you an interview, make an effort to show up looking well put together. If you show up for an interview wearing clothes that fitted you perfectly in the pre-paunch 1980s, with evidence of that morning's breakfast mingling with your ZZ Top beard, not to mention smelling gently of last night's garlic bread and sporting a hairstyle borrowed from Tom Hanks in the latter stages of *Castaway*, you can pretty much kiss that job good-bye.

If you're in the mood for more "don't do" stuff, brace yourself for IDEA 10, *The seven deadly resumé sins.*

Try another idea...

"If you're thinking of finding a new job, it's worth knowing that only 7 percent of those recruiting staff look favorably on resumés with quirky features such as photos or humor. So play it straight."
JULIA FEUELL, Managing Director of New Frontiers

Defining idea...

How did it go?

Q   I can't decide whether my resumé needs to be more eye-catching or more conservative. Do you have any tips?

A   You've put your finger on the great resumé paradox. How can your resumé stand out from the competition without standing out so much that employers will get nervous about you? Actually, there is no paradox really: If you want to stand out in a crowd, by all means don a clown's outfit; if you want your resumé to stand out in a recruiter's eyes, concentrate on professional, well-presented content rather than colored paper and presentational gimmickry.

Q   Actually, I consider myself something of a character. In fact, people tell me I'm larger than life. Shouldn't that come through in my resumé?

A   It's your choice, of course. At one level I'm all for being authentic when it comes to resumés. If we sat in a bath of cold beans for charity a couple of years ago, why shouldn't the recruitment world know? If we send all our personal correspondence out accompanied by tiny glittery stars that scatter all over the floor when the envelope is opened, why shackle our style when we apply for jobs? Unfortunately, employers tend to respond to conservatism in a resumé, not flamboyance, and the plain facts are that resumés with "character" have a lower success rate in terms of interview invitations than their "does what it says on the package" counterparts. Reflect your outrageous self in your resumé by all means, but be aware that as a direct consequence you'll likely have to wait a while for an employer to come along who is prepared to take on the full-on, unexpurgated, bean-dripping you.

18

Surfing resumés

A reminder that job searching has gone digital.

Those of you in your forties or fifties with a disdain for new technology had better be warned that there's a generation of Internet-savvy, technologically hip people coming through who may well turn out to be the reason why you don't get your next promotion or job offer.

It's estimated that up to 80 percent of medium to large organizations use some form of electronic scanning system to process resumés. Additionally, there are a growing number of smaller companies that buy in recruitment services from external providers who in turn make use of scanning systems. Add to that the huge growth in online recruitment services and you've got a significant portion of the recruitment market where the first sift and cut of resumés is put together by an unfeeling machine as opposed to somebody from Personnel (apparently, there's a difference between the two).

Here's an idea for you...

Use both general and specific keywords. For example, if the recruiting organization is looking for somebody who is comfortable using standard business software packages, it's worthwhile listing both Microsoft Office as a generic name and the specific programs like Microsoft Word, Excel, PowerPoint, and so on.

HOW ELECTRONIC SCANNING WORKS

Think of electronic scanning as a three-step process:

Step 1 On arrival, a resumé is fed through a scanner and then converted into a readable file.

Step 2 The computer rummages through the file for keywords (i.e., relevant skills, experience, knowledge, abilities, and education) and places the resumé in an appropriate database.

Step 3 When a vacancy arises, the employer uses an applicant tracking system to locate and extract the resumés that contain the keywords associated with the role being filled.

This matching process works effectively when matching people with "hard" skills, and so the individuals who are popular on databases are people in professions like engineering, computer science, finance, accounting, marketing, management, and human resources. Anybody working in "softer" areas like fashion design or the visual arts may find that their experience doesn't suit this medium.

TACTICS FOR SURVIVING THE CUT

How does the fact that a significant chunk of the recruitment market now uses electronic resumé databases to search for people with specific experience and qualifications impact the way in which we put our resumés together?

Well, the most important thing is to make sure that we include the right keywords in our resumé. For this reason, it's best to describe our experience with concrete words rather than vague descriptions.

To ensure that your resumé goes through a scanner as productively as possible, remember the following:

1. Use white 8½ by 11 paper for best results; definitely avoid tinted paper as this can significantly undermine the scanner's character-reading capability.

2. Print on one side only.

3. Provide a laser-printed original for the best results. A typewritten original or a high-quality photocopy are also OK. Avoid dot-matrix printouts (you still have a dot-matrix printer...?) and low-quality photocopies.

4. Don't fold or staple the pages.

Specialist recruiters are geared up to keep you doing what you've always been doing. Is that what you want? Remind yourself with another peek at IDEA 1, *Dream a little dream.*

Try another idea...

83

5. Use standard typefaces. Avoid fancy styles such as italics, underline, shadows, and reverses (white letters on black background). Definitely avoid typefaces where the letters touch each other as character-reading software really struggles to interpret this.

6. Use a font size of no less than 10 points and no bigger than 14 points.

7. Avoid gimmicks like a two-column format or presenting your resumé in the form of a newspaper or newsletter.

You need to ensure that your resumé looks the part for both electronic and human scanning. There are still plenty of organizations where electronic scanning isn't used and so you need to cover all the angles. In other words, you need to use keywords in your resumé while also ensuring that it still looks easy on the eye.

Oh, and one final point. Electronic scanning is another reason why you really must make sure that you avoid typos. For example, if "Excel" is a keyword and you've spelled it "Exsel," then the vast majority of scanning systems would have you logged as somebody with no Excel experience.

"The medium is the message."
MARSHALL McLUHAN

Q **I've tried including keywords. My resumé looks OK, but how can I be sure that I have the right keywords?**

How did it go?

A *You're right to be concerned. Coming up with the right keywords is a must. The secret is to be as concrete and specific as possible with your language. The good news is that electronic scanning systems don't penalize you for including too many keywords, only for failing to identify the right ones. For that reason, feel uninhibited about including terms that you feel just might be relevant. Remember as well that if the original job listing has done its job, most of the relevant keywords shouldn't be that hard to identify.*

Q **How can I include all the keywords I want without making my resumé look messy and cluttered to the human eye?**

A *That's fairly straightforward. Include as many keywords as you can in the natural flow of the resumé and then put the rest in a section named "Key Competencies" and your resumé will still look OK aesthetically.*

19

Dollars and sense

Avoid giving details of your salary on your resumé. If you're specifically asked to do so, however, here are some tips on how to go about it.

In a perfect job-hunting world, your current salary will nuzzle a perfect thousand or two below the starting salary outlined in the advertisement for your next potential position.

But how do you play things if you either earn a lot more or a lot less than the stated salary range in a job listing you'd like to respond to and you're asked to give details of your current salary?

This situation can easily arise. Perhaps you earn a fortune in your current job and don't want to price yourself out of the market. Or maybe you have a pension coming in and therefore don't need to maintain your current salary level. Or your current company is in a notoriously low-paying sector.

DON'T SHOW THEM THE MONEY

In my opinion, a direct answer to the salary question will hurt your chances. Think about it. A typical job posting in something like the *New York Times* can generate

Here's an idea for you...

If you feel that your new employer might struggle to match your current salary, develop a package of non-salary elements that could form an alternative negotiating package. Such elements could include flexible working, vacation entitlement, education assistance, car, laptop, professional organization membership, gym fees, health insurance, and severance package.

literally hundreds of resumés. One of the easier ways in which that poor sap in the personnel department can whittle down numbers is to weed out any applicants who are too expensive and therefore quite possibly overqualified. The same goes for applicants whose salaries are too low, implying that that they might be underqualified.

Though it's tempting to do so, don't simply ignore the request for salary information. If the advertisement specifically requests a response, not providing one will have you labeled by the recruiter as either rude (because you didn't bother to respond) or someone with poor attention to detail (because you didn't notice the reference to salary information). Neither of those labels is going to have you waltzing into an interview.

Consider including one of the following explanations in your cover letter (you should always keep salary information away from your resumé):

- "My salary requirements are negotiable."
- "My salary history is consistent with my experience and record of achievements."
- "My salary consists of a number of elements, including a performance-related payment. I will be happy to talk these through in more detail at a meeting."

By giving some kind of response, you've shown that you've read the ad, even if you're choosing to evade the issue. Most recruitment consultants and HR managers that I know tell me that they wouldn't take offense at any of the responses above. Actually, one HR contact told me that any of those replies would give them one less reason not to call the applicant.

Salary isn't the only area where you can scuttle your chances of getting an interview if you play it wrong. Check out IDEA 21, *Detox your resumé.*

Try another idea...

TALKING SALARY FACE-TO-FACE

If your response on salary has satisfied the recruiter and they like the look of your experience and qualifications, there's more than a fighting chance that you'll get an interview. Having bought yourself a little time in terms of the salary question, you can think about how to play things when you're face-to-face with the interviewer.

First things first. If the interviewer doesn't raise the subject of salary, then you shouldn't either. Presenting yourself in the interview is a sales process, whereas talking salary is a negotiation process. Trying to sell yourself and negotiate simultaneously weakens your bargaining hand. Sell yourself in the interview and subsequently get a job offer; then you've got a very strong buying signal from the company and you can negotiate from a position of real strength.

However, if the question of the salary you require does arise, you can try saying that you'd like to make as much as other employees with your qualifications. Or you could try answering the question with a question like, "What is a typical salary for this position?" Another alternative is to respond by giving a pay range rather than a specific figure.

"Why is there so much month left at the end of the money?"
JOHN BARRYMORE, actor

Defining idea...

89

And if you're pressed to give details of your current salary, you have a number of options. If you're trying to play down your current rate then consider simply giving them your basic salary. If you need to increase the value of your package then you could give a number that encapsulates everything down to the lunch vouchers.

How did it go?

Q   I've found my perfect next job. It pays quite a bit less than I currently make, but I've got a little pension and a few dollars coming in from investments so I can afford the drop. Any further tips regarding how I should play things?

A   *If they expressly ask what you currently make, give them the absolute basic rate. If that's still too high, you can add that your previous company was noted for paying well above the market rate. You could also pitch the line that the salary offered is only one consideration in taking a position— opportunities for personal and career development, cutting down commuting time, or maybe flexible work hours are just as important.*

Q   What if my perfect job didn't turn out to be so perfect after all and I wanted to look for a job at my former higher salary. How would I play the salary question then?

A   *There's no foolproof way out of this one. I'd recommend telling them openly that you took a job that didn't pan out and that the experience has confirmed to you that your former work was what you really love and what you're really best at. Then cross your fingers and hope that your previous track record is good enough to outweigh this slight career aberration.*

20

Reference points

I'm sure you can rustle up two people who would write something vaguely complimentary about you. Even so, manage the process; don't leave it to chance.

The South African golfer Gary Player was once asked whether he thought he was lucky on the golf course. "Yes," he reportedly answered, "and the more I practice the luckier I get."

There's a clear message here for all aspiring job-changers: To get the best results, leave as little to chance as possible. For most of the process of putting a resumé together, control is very much in our own hands. We choose the format, determine the content and style, and decide who to send it to.

Typically, though, when it comes to providing the names of references to potential employers, we can find ourselves resorting to giving the contact details of a complete stranger, all too often a no-name pencil pusher in the personnel department.

Here's an idea for you...

Make it clear to colleagues past and present that you're very happy to provide a reference for them. This will both earn you their gratitude and help you to keep tabs on who is moving where. In so doing you'll provide yourself with a range of networking contacts in different organizations.

But is this really the best person you can come up with to impress the next prospective payer of your salary? Possibly not. Unless that person knows you personally, chances are they'll pass the reference request to one of their admin team who will dig out your file from the archives during a quiet moment. Apart from confirming the dates you worked for the company and maybe providing details of your sick record while employed there, the best you're likely to get out of that administrator is a bland, noncommittal "know of no reason why the candidate should not be hired" reference. Not damaging, admittedly, but no glowing testimonial either. So, how can we sort the referential wheat from the chaff?

Most potential employers still make a point of seeking written references before confirming a job offer. Therefore, it's worth putting a little effort into identifying people who are well placed to comment positively on you and the contribution you have made. Ideally, have a range of possible references on hand so that you can give the most appropriate set of names to the company that wants to take you on.

Defining idea...

"I can live for two months on a good compliment."
MARK TWAIN

What will clinch a good reference for you, though, isn't so much the people you choose, but how well you manage your dealings with those individuals. I've had requests for references pop through the mailbox from time to time for people who I've worked with or known in the past.

There's more on developing contacts in IDEA 22, *Perfect your personal elevator pitch.*

Try another idea…

Call me Mr. Grumpy if you like, but I object to these requests just showing up out of the blue. In my mind, there's a certain etiquette to be followed here. Before naming anybody as a reference, I'd recommend making contact with them to ensure that they're happy to provide a reference. And remember that although the details of your time working with that individual may be etched in your brain, your reference may not remember your precise job title, the dates that you worked with them, or indeed some of your specific achievements. For that reason, it makes good sense to let them have a copy of your resumé so that they can refresh their memory. Depending on the relationship you have with your reference, you might even want to supply a draft reference that they might care to use. This way, you can be assured of a positive write-up. You've also reestablished a connection with somebody who might be a very useful networking contact at some point in the future.

"If you want to win friends, make it a point to remember them. If you remember my name, you pay me a subtle compliment; you indicate that I have made an impression on you. Remember my name and you add to my feeling of importance."
DALE CARNEGIE

Defining idea…

How did it go?

Q **I supplied references to my new employer some time ago, but I spoke last night to one of the people I named as a reference and they haven't heard anything. What should I do?**

A *Unless you're the new HR director, nothing! It's the employer's responsibility to contact references. If they choose not to do so or forget to ask, then it's not your problem. If you are the new HR director, then it's time to put a rocket under your recruitment people and remind them that references are one of the primary tools available to the organization to find out if candidates have told the truth about themselves.*

Q **I've been told that my last employer refuses to supply references for any of their employees. Can that be right?**

A *Yes, an employer can refuse to provide a reference. There is no statutory duty to provide an existing employee or ex-employee with a reference. The vast majority of employers, however, will supply references on request from a legitimate source.*

Q **I supplied details of a personal reference, but I've been told that this isn't acceptable. Is this normal?**

A *References are usually sought from current and former employers. Some companies take the view that information from personal references is of low value.*

21

Detox your resumé

Draw out any harmful content that might raise negative thoughts in the mind of the recruiter.

You don't get two chances to make a first impression. Usually a potential employer will only have your resumé (plus maybe a cover letter) on which to base their impression of you.

It's therefore only natural for you to want your resumé to look as good as it possibly can. And part of that is about only including information that will make a positive impact on the employer. The reverse side of that particular coin is to excise any information that is likely to have a negative impact on the employer.

Here are a few things that your resumé will be better off without:

STRIP OUT SURPLUS CONTENT

We've already established that resumés are one-to-one marketing documents. They're about accentuating the positive. Applying for a job isn't the time to strip yourself naked before the resumé jury and reveal yourself warts and all. Employers might appreciate your searing honesty, but you'll be unlikely to land an interview.

Here's an idea for you... **Use spell-check, but remember it won't catch every error. An unnerving example is that if you left the "l" out of "public relations," spell-check will happily nod that through, but the PR director with the vacancy might be less forgiving!**

Sometimes knowing what to cut out of your resumé is a matter of common sense, but sometimes it's a bit more of a judgment call.

In the common-sense category comes all the gratuitous information, i.e., information you've not been asked explicitly to provide that is likely to do your cause more harm than good if you include it. For example, an obsession with extreme sports might keep your stocks of adrenaline high, but it'll probably cause employers concern. Likewise, mentioning the penalty points you have on your driving license can only have a negative impact. Or listing your personal website if it happens to contain pictures of you mooning the camera.

In the judgment call terrain, matters aren't quite so clear-cut. It's more about tone and nuance. Here's an example: Let's say that you're applying for a role that's 100 percent about dealing with customers face to face. Describing the face-to-face element of your current role ought therefore to get the recruiter's interest. If you devote, say, two bullet points out of four to this facet of your job, it will come across as a substantive part of what you do. However, if those two bullets are out of eight bullets, then you're beginning to dilute their impact by implying that you spend a lot of your time in non-customer-facing activity. Should you place the two bullets in the middle or toward the bottom of the eight, then that will diminish their effect further.

CLEAN UP SPELLING ERRORS

Employers have a nasty habit of assuming that anybody who makes a spelling mistake in their resumé is likely to make mistakes on the job. At the very least, you're guilty of a lack of attention to detail.

The following bloopers were all taken from real resumés and cover letters:

- I am very detail-oreinted.
- Graduated in the top 66 percent of my class.
- Special skills: Thyping.
- Objection: To utilize my skills in sales.
- I am a rabid typist.
- Skills: Operated Pitney Bones machine.
- Strengths: Ability to meet deadlines while maintaining composer.
- Work Experience: Dealing with customers' conflicts that arouse.
- Typing Speed: 756 wpm.

DETOX YOUR QUIRKY INDIVIDUALITY

No photo, no wacky fonts, no colored paper, no jokes, no eccentric hobbies, no exclamation marks, no personal pronouns, no "Resumé" at the top of each page, no volunteered salary details, no mention of political affiliation, no early schooling details, and no unnecessary repetition of facts.

Try another idea...

Having de-accentuated the negative, maybe it's time to build up the positive aspects of your resumé. Have a look at IDEA 5, *Learn to speak "behaviorese."*

Defining idea...

"The key to any game is to use your strengths and hide your weaknesses."
PAUL WESTPHAL, former basketball player

How did it go?

Q **I think I've stripped out all of the damaging content, but how can I be sure?**

A   *In a world that's constantly changing it's hard to be certain that you've excised every last hint of damaging content, but a good starting point is to get someone else to read your resumé specifically with an eye out for errors. However, be aware that they, too, might not spot errors like "manger" in place of "manager" because we're inclined to read what we think should be there rather than what actually is there.*

Q **I'm happy that I've fixed any typing errors, but what about detoxing the rest of the content?**

A   *Read your resumé again. Go through it line by line and ask yourself whether each bit of information is relevant to the role you've applied for, deleting anything that fails the test. Then ask yourself whether the information is presented in the right order, with the appropriate weight given to each point. Remember that the more important the information, the nearer to the top of the resumé it should be. Any highly relevant information on page two of your resumé probably deserves a promotion.*

22

Perfect your personal elevator pitch

How to use your resumé as a basis for developing a succinct and memorable personal "commercial" that will register you positively with other people.

Let's face it, the question on everyone's lips on meeting somebody for the first time is more often than not, "So what do you do?"

There we are, say, at a party or a wedding and one of the first ways we try to pin down the person we're talking to is to find out what they do for a living. In these more egalitarian times, we're not necessarily that bothered about whether we're talking with a captain of industry or a plumber—we just want to know. Perhaps, like me, however, you've occasionally been at the receiving end of a brain-numbingly dull answer to that question, where the only point of interest is how long you can last before that oops-there-goes-my-will-to-live moment.

Here are a few pointers for when you first meet someone:

1. Smile. Not too fleetingly (can seem insincere) or for too long (can look a tad manic).

Don't try to define yourself too literally. International speaker and networking guru Roy Sheppard believes that we need to go well beyond our job titles and identify what results we create. Consider the difference between saying "I'm a professional one-on-one career coach" and "I help people build better careers and lives for themselves."

2. Offer your right hand positively to invite a handshake. This is generally a good idea, but don't bother if the other party has a plate in one hand and a drink in the other.

3. Always expect to offer your name first when kicking off a conversation. People like to know who they're talking with and will generally tell you who they are in return. If you come across somebody and you think you've met before, still offer your name first to put them at ease (they might be struggling to remember your name).

4. If somebody else introduces you to an acquaintance of theirs, make sure you're happy with the way they did it. For example, following an introduction along the lines of "And this old reprobate is my drinking buddy John, who claims to be a writer," you might want to chime in with something a little more formal.

You now have the chance to offer up some conversational bait to make a positive impression on the other person. You can make something up on the spot if you wish, but if you really want to impress, don't rely on your ability to spontaneously come up with a compelling self-description.

Instead, I'd recommend that you try to come up with a short (30 seconds or less), sharp, and interesting way of describing yourself. Take the time to write down your answer and then take the time to read it. Your aim is to light up the eyes of a prospective client or command a vote of confidence from a satisfied past client. If your self-introduction makes you yawn, then you can expect to bore the pants off all the people you meet, too. So, it's worth giving this some serious thought and making a serious effort to imagine and develop yourself as a brand.

Meeting people is one thing. Using those connections to your advantage is another. IDEA 20, *Reference points*, provides advice on how to choose the right reference.

Try another idea...

You might want to start by identifying the qualities or characteristics that make you distinctive from your competitors and even your colleagues. What would people (colleagues, customers, etc.) say is your greatest strength or your most noteworthy personal trait? To put the challenge succinctly, ask yourself what you want to be known for. Work out the answer to that and you'll be well on the way to creating your elevator pitch.

"If you think of your resumé as an elevator pitch—the kind of punchy and concise delivery you have to give when you're selling something—you begin to realize that the formal list of jobs and qualifications to which we have become accustomed needs to be reordered."
BILL FAUST, author of *Pitch Yourself*

Defining idea...

101

How did it go?

Q **I tried my elevator pitch the other day and it was a disaster. I'm not at all comfortable with the idea. Besides, I work at home! Is it really worth it?**

A *I'm detecting a bit of resistance here! The idea of proclaiming what makes us so good to a partial or complete stranger doesn't always come naturally. Nevertheless, like any new habit, it will become more comfortable the more you do it. Funnily enough, we often have more trouble giving our pitch to an individual than to a group of individuals. I suspect that when we introduce ourselves to a group, there's more of a performance element involved, which in turn makes us feel a little less personally exposed.*

Q **I'm now comfortable with giving my pitch to groups, but I still stumble a little when I'm talking one on one. Do you have any more suggestions?**

A *The first option is to practice, practice, practice, practice. Practice in front of a mirror. Practice into a voice recorder. Just try to make it a perfectly workaday thing in your life. Eventually you'll shift from being consciously incompetent to being unconsciously competent! The second option is to slightly change the way you launch your elevator pitch. The next time somebody wants to know who you are and what you do, simply kick off with, "What I normally tell people who ask that question is that . . ." and then slip into your pitch. Sounds bizarre I know, but it means that instead of delivering your pitch directly to somebody, you're putting your response in quotation marks. Many people I know feel more comfortable with this.*

23

Manage the brand called You

A unique selling point will make you stand out from the crowd. So, what makes you so special?

What particular combination of skills and experience might give you an edge over others going for the same job?

"It's this simple: You are a brand. You are in charge of your brand. There is no single path to success. And there is no one right way to create the brand called You. Except this: Start today. Or else."

That's a quote from Tom Peters, probably the world's best-known (and best-paid) management guru, in an article called "The Brand Called You: You Can't Move Up If You Don't Stand Out" that he wrote for *Fast Company* magazine in August 1997. In a nutshell, the article proposed that we should manage our career as though it were a brand. Peters proposed that like a classic marketing brand, our personal brand value can rise or fall depending on how well we nurture and manage our brand and how well we perform in the marketplace.

Here's an idea for you...

Ask yourself the following deceptively simple question to help you define your brand: What do I want to be famous for? Then ask yourself what needs to happen next in order for you to get closer to your chosen brand identity.

But this isn't just a concept to apply to people with a high media profile. You may cringe at the thought of being "a brand called You" or "Chief Executive of Me," but behind this clodhopping language rests a new truth about what lays ahead for everyone looking to change jobs.

To put it bluntly, getting a new job isn't the challenge. Finding the right job is, however. Whether you're contemplating an internal or external move, you need to make sure that it keeps your career moving in an upward trajectory. Choose the right employer and that can increase your brand value. Choose the wrong employer and you can do lasting damage to your earning potential.

So, what can we do to protect our careers?

ACTIVELY MANAGE YOUR CAREER

I can sympathize if reading this stuff is making you feel exhausted, but please don't be like most of your colleagues, who probably manage their careers on the fly. The trouble is, the general assumption seems to be that performing well in a given job is all that matters. In other words, look after your job and somehow your career will take care of itself. Not true. Building a long and successful career requires a "planned maintenance" mentality. Don't assume that combining patience with a dollop of opportunism will do the trick—nothing comes to those who wait. Or

Defining idea...

"In a nutshell, the key to success is identifying unique modules of talent within you and then finding the right arena in which to use them."
WARREN BENNIS, author and social philosopher

to quote my favorite Chinese proverb: "A peasant must stand a long time on a hillside with his mouth wide open before a roast duck flies in."

KEEP YOUR HANDS ON THE WHEEL

Don't entrust your career to anybody. Don't rely on the company's Management Development Manager or VP-Succession Planning to look after your interests—they have other fish to fry. And don't rely on your current boss to look after your best interests. Now I admit that I may be doing them a grave disservice, but all too many managers are very happy to keep their good people for as long as they possibly can.

Here's the acid test: Has your boss ever said anything to you along the lines of "I'm concerned that you're not spending enough time planning your next job move. You should be keeping an eye out for the right opportunity. Oh, and start networking more"? Paradoxically, if your boss has been saying that to you, it's probably because they think you're awful at your job and they're desperate to shuffle you off the premises.

AIM HIGH

Finally, don't imagine that the skills, knowledge, and experience that got you where you are today will be sufficient to propel you where you want to be in the future. Seek out opportunities to acquire new skills, become a voracious learner, and develop career purpose. People with a vision of their future and goals linked to that vision are far more likely to succeed than those without.

Try another idea...

Have another look at IDEA 4, *Cut to the chase*, to help you assess whether your resumé trumpets your brand. You might also want to have a look at IDEA 5, *Learn to speak "behaviorese,"* if you feel your resumé needs an injection of energy.

Defining idea...

"You don't have an old-fashioned résumé anymore! You've got a marketing brochure for brand You."
TOM PETERS, management guru

105

How did it go?

Q **I'm struggling to put this idea into practice. Can you provide a few practical pointers on how I can build my brand value?**

A *Personal brand building happens over months and years rather than days and weeks. You'll need to commit quite a bit of time and energy to the process. In a magazine article, Tom Peters gave five tips:*

1. ***Find a mentor****: Time was when mentors used to pick their protégés; these days, protégés are likely to be picking their mentors.*

2. ***Look the part****: Dress in a style that suits your job, and that matches people's expectations.*

3. ***Become an active member of your professional association****: It will increase your professional know-how and help you build an impressive set of contacts.*

4. ***Specialize****: Be the person that everybody turns to when the budget needs checking, or the computer goes wrong, or when people want a good listener.*

5. ***Develop your presentation skills.***

Q **These all seem like useful short-term steps to take, but what about in the longer term?**

A *The most important thing is to have a vision: Think hard about your goals and how you're going to achieve them.*

24

One last thing (20 actually)

Use this checklist to ensure that you send your resumé out in good shape.

Let's assume that you've absorbed what you will from the previous ideas, seen the job of your dreams, and had a crack at putting together a resumé that will blow the recruiter's socks off.

Just before you seal your resumé in the envelope and head off to the mailbox, why not refer to this twenty-item checklist that is intended to help reassure you that your resumé is as good as it could be. See how yours measures up in its current state.

1. Have you researched the position you're applying for as well as you possibly can? Is your research reflected in the content of your resumé?

2. Double-check that all your contact details are up to date. Make sure you've given a cell phone number and your email address. If your email is something like fluffybunnyinboobooland362436@hotmail.com, consider changing it for something that sounds a tad more professional.

Make a list of your career priorities for the next six months. Then put an entry in your diary for six months from today, marking it something like "Personal Review," and on that date allow yourself at least a couple of hours to take stock of how you're doing. Make this an ongoing process.

3. Does your profile statement explicitly target the job you're applying for?

4. Have you provided evidence to back up anything you've said about yourself in your profile?

5. Have you quantified the information in your resumé as much as possible?

6. Have you put your achievements in order of relevance and significance to fit the job you're applying for?

7. Have you used terminology that people outside your present company will understand?

8. Check that you've avoided jargon, acronyms, and abbreviations where possible.

9. Does your resumé look balanced? Have you put the emphasis on your most recent career with diminishing levels of detail as you go back in time to earlier roles? Remember that corporate pre-history began about six years ago.

10. Does your resumé sound upbeat? Does it read as though you are enthusiastic about tackling the job?

11. Are you confident that you could talk through any aspect of your resumé if it came up at an interview? Eliminate any content that you may feel uncomfortable discussing.

Close your eyes and pick a page, any page. Whichever idea you land on, it *will* be relevant.

Try another idea...

12. Double-check any dates. There are a surprising number of resumés in circulation where people managed to start a job in 2003 and leave it in 2001.

13. Make sure that you have given the reference for the job you are applying for and where you saw that job posting.

14. Have you provided all the information that the job listing specified, such as salary details, dates available for interview, etc.?

15. Check for typos. Sounds obvious, I know, but it's so easy to let a phew slip though the net. Don't rely on your software package's spell-checker—the number of senior "mangers" that show up on resumés is staggering.

"Successful job hunting is a learned skill. You have to study it. You have to practice it. You have to master it, just like any new skill. And master it thoroughly because you'll need it all the rest of your life."
RICHARD BOLLES, career guru and author of *What Color Is Your Parachute?*

Defining idea...

16. Have you used good-quality paper and a good printer for your resumé and cover letter? If it's an application form, have you completed it in black ink to ensure that it will photocopy well?

17. Have you asked somebody to look through your resumé?

18. Put your application into an envelope and send it out by first-class mail.

19. Feel free to add anything to the checklist that strikes you as helpful.

20. If you haven't been doing so already, from now on keep an ongoing note of your achievements at work and any job changes so that you're prepared for when you next need to go through this entire process.

I think that's about it. Good luck! Let me know how you do.

How did it go?

Q   I've just handed in my notice to my current employers. Do you have any tips on exiting with style?

A   *When it comes to handing in your notice, remember that the way we leave a company speaks volumes about us. So leave with good grace: Buy the doughnuts and maybe a round of drinks; go around the office and personally say good-bye to the people you liked as well as any others who you'd like to speak well of you; and whatever you do, don't lace any* farewell speeches with vitriol—you're not going to endear yourself to your soon-to-be former colleagues by telling them what losers they are for staying there.

Q **Tomorrow is my first day in my new job. How should I play things?**

A *Bear in mind that your new boss, colleagues, and team, possibly the whole organization, will be watching you in the early days. First impressions count. Here are a few tips on how to prolong the honeymoon period:*

- *Be visible. Get out and meet as many people as possible.*

- *Find out who's who, get a handle on company policies and procedures. Absorb as much as you can as quickly as you can.*

- *Don't refer to your former organization as "we"; in fact, only ever refer to your past experience if it's relevant in some way.*

- *Be guarded about your views. There will be plenty of organizational hot potatoes and people will be trying to recruit you to their various causes or grievances.*

- *Make something happen as soon as you can. If 100 days have gone by and the impression people have is that little if anything has changed, then you've missed the boat.*

Knockout
Interview Answers

25

What interests you about our particular industry?

Some interviewers are better than others. Good ones use open questions like this one to open you up and get you talking. Poorer ones fall into the trap of asking closed questions. Look out for open questions—you want them because they give you the chance to make your points.

Recognizing an open question helps you to understand how in principle you're going to give them answers that knock their socks off and it can even help you to give a good answer to a bad question.

Overheard at a sales training course:

Rookie salesperson: "I'm not quite getting this. Could you just give me an example of an open question?"

Trainer: "Why?"

Rookie salesperson: "Because maybe I'll understand an example better than I understand the theory."

Trainer: "Why?"
Rookie salesperson: "Oh, this is getting so frustrating! Why don't you just give me an example?"
Trainer: "Ah, now that's a good question."

Here is the single-word open question, "Why," doing its job beautifully. Although the rookie doesn't yet understand what an open question is, she does exactly what the questioner wants. The questioner makes the person answering give honest and instinctive answers.

Here's an idea for you...

Have a conversation with some colleagues or friends in which you only ask open questions. Try to do as little of the talking as you possibly can. Ask them questions about themselves, their families, their interests, and so on. You'll be surprised how easy it is to get them talking and opening up about themselves. There are two benefits to doing this exercise. One is that you will appreciate what a skilled interviewer is trying to do and the second is that it makes you listen, another great interview skill.

DISPLAYING KNOWLEDGE IN ANSWERING OPEN QUESTIONS

"What interests you about our industry?" is an open question. It requires you to reveal what you know about the business the organization is in and why you are interested in being involved in it. So be prepared. A poor answer to this question, particularly one that demonstrates that you don't know anything about the industry or the organization, is a showstopper that'll get you off to the poorest possible start. In fact, many people regard it as quite rude for an interviewee not to have done such basic research.

Good interviewers use a "funnel" technique in their questioning. They start with a very open question and then funnel down deeper and deeper into specifics. So, it's always dangerous to say anything that you can't substantiate or expand on.

If possible, tie your interest in the industry into an interest you've had from an early age. You will see further relevance of this in IDEA 16, *My hobbies are Ping-Pong, playing the ukulele, and going to the theater.*

Try another idea...

It's easy enough nowadays to brief yourself on an industry using the Internet. Look not only at the website of the organization you're thinking of joining but also at their main competitors. Look for how fast the industry is growing, how profitable it is, and how much change has occurred in recent years. All of these investigations lead you to a good answer. You can be interested in the business no matter what state it is in. "I want to take part in the rapid growth and change that is taking place in the telecommunications industry. I'm excited about being involved in a rapidly changing market where you have to be very light on your feet to keep up with the competition." Or alternatively, "The food-retailing industry is very interesting because over many years you've developed very detailed and sophisticated answers to all the tough business problems such as branding, planned discounting, and so on. I think I can learn most and quickest in such an environment."

"I keep six honest serving men (They taught me all I knew) Their names are What and Why and When And How and Where and Who."
RUDYARD KIPLING

Defining idea...

Another good source of information is the company's annual report. Look at the mission statement and try to find out why you want to be involved with an organization with this particular stated aim. Quote from a recent newspaper article to show that you're taking an interest. (If it's a big organization then go into any newspaper site and search for the name of the company. If it's smaller then use a search engine and you'll probably come up with something.)

USING WELL-PREPARED ANSWERS

The industry sector will come up in some way whether they ask the question this way or not, so it's good technique to have the actual words you're going to use in your head before you go in. In fact, all the preparation you've done in this area will help at some point in the interview. It just shows that you're interested in being a part of the business that, after all, the interviewer is giving a large chunk of their working life to.

Now think about the question as asked by a less skilled interviewer: "Are you interested in our industry?" This is an easy closed question—as if you're going to say, "No, I'd much rather be in showbiz!" Answer it as though it were an open one. In fact, it's the same answer with a slightly different starting point.

Q I tried this at a recent interview where I didn't get the job: I used some knowledge of their industry, including the phrase "strategic partnerships," a term I got from their annual report. He came back asking what I meant by the term and I tried to explain but clearly looked out of my depth. That's the danger of this technique, isn't it? They'll see through your scant knowledge.

How did it go?

A *Try not to bluff them in an area where they obviously know tons more than you. Think about possible follow-up questions and then when you use some of their jargon finish by asking them what they mean by the term. "I see your strategy revolves around 'strategic partnerships.' Can you tell me what that phrase means in this particular organization?"*

Q In an interview I just went to I asked the interviewer some open questions. She then went on for about ten minutes without asking me a question. That doesn't give me a chance to convey to her how I'm right for the job, does it?

A *Possibly not, but in the grand majority of cases people most enjoy conversations if they've done most of the talking. Relax and let them talk themselves into hiring you.*

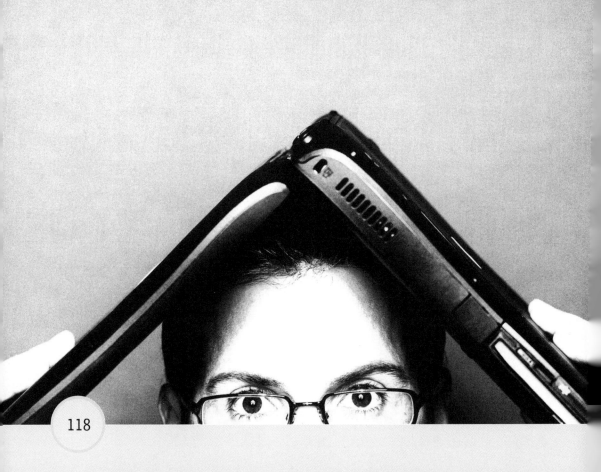

26

What makes you a good leader?

The HR people will probably interview you at some point. Even if they don't you can bet that they're talking to the other interviewers behind the scenes. Understanding what they're looking for gives you a competitive edge.

Human resources managers have "degrees in people" and they're looking for talent, not just someone to do this job. They want people who'll do this job well and have potential for the future.

You can pretty much sum up the HR, or personnel, interest at an interview in terms of leadership skills. They want to know how you will shape up if you're given the tricky job of leading a team in their organization. So before we look at good answers to the question "What makes you a good leader?" let's agree on what they're probing for and what leadership is. Let's start from what it's not:

Team member to non-leader:	"Sorry to bother you but I've got a problem at home. My mother-in-law is staying with us and she's starting to make life impossible for my wife."
Non-leader:	"That's not a problem. My wife wants a divorce; now that's a problem!"

The old cliché is true: The best communicators are listeners. Leaders always concentrate on the interests of their people. In fact, a good leader may very well know a lot more about you than you do about them.

THIS QUESTION IS ABSOLUTELY ABOUT YOU

Leadership capabilities are the attributes that make you successful; your personal attributes, if you like, or what you are naturally good at. Human resources managers are looking at your character as well as your innate ability to manage people and influence how they go about their jobs. Leadership also has to do with energy and getting things done. Many organizations asking a question in this area are also probing for the values that a person brings to the workplace. Everyone needs leadership skills and drive, whether they manage people or not. They're trying to answer the question, "Can this person achieve success by influencing other people inside and outside the organization?"

Here's an idea for you...

Look at your last appraisal. Is there anything there you can use as proof that someone else has noted your natural abilities in the leadership area? It's always more powerful to quote someone else than point out, modestly of course, how brilliant you think you are.

So plan your answer to include a number of these attributes and try to prove them with evidence or example as well as by simple assertion. A safe place to start is two of the key attributes of a natural leader—resilience and flexibility. "I find that I am generally the first person in my team to recover after a setback and generate the idea that starts to get us back on track." This is a good double-pronged answer showing resilience and your ability to create new ideas. "A good manager I worked for once demonstrated to me how important it is to be flexible in how you handle people. She treated everyone as unique individuals and got the best out of us in different ways."

IDEA 35, *What is the one thing your team would most like to change about you?*, gives further clues on leading people, listening to them and responding to their needs.

Try another idea...

Your "values" as a leader are a little more tricky. You'll probably demonstrate your values as you go through the interview, but if you want to use an open question like this to make the point, the safest way is to link it to the research you did on the organization. "On your website you talk about 'quality driving everything we do' and that attracted me. I've always been competitive and I like to do things properly." Be careful with this one, though; don't lay it on with a trowel. "Values" is an area where the candidate can be a bit soupy or insincere. The key is to interpret particular values and make sense of them within your job.

TRUST ME, I'M A LEADER

Perhaps the most difficult element of this question is the assertion that people can trust you. You can only do this by example. Try telling them what you did to gain the trust of the team you're working with currently. Or do it the harder way of talking about behavior from a member of your team that you regarded as inappropriate; what did you say and do about it? This is another double-pronged answer because it demonstrates that the organization can trust you and the values you work within.

"The final test of leaders is that they leave behind them in other people the conviction and the will to carry on."
WALTER LIPPMANN, journalist

Defining idea...

121

How did it go?

Q **I'm going for an internal promotion, and I really know what you mean about "values" and people being mawkish about them. Top management has just produced a new version of our values and everyone is mouthing off about them in a way that I can't because it sounds like so much management-speak. I'll have to talk about them, though, because they are very much the flavor of the month. Do you think that's all right?**

A *Try saying just that to them: "I have a slight concern that people are learning the words of the new values but not necessarily demonstrating them. This makes me a bit uncomfortable." This could lead to a good discussion. Keep an eye on the HR person's reactions when you try this, though.*

Q **They asked me to tell them about a time when I had ignored company procedures because I felt that they were impeding my ability to complete a project. I thought it was a trick question and told them that I felt the procedures were there for a purpose and would not normally have such an effect. My instincts immediately told me that this wasn't a good answer. Were they right?**

A *Yes, afraid so. Organizations expect leaders to take risks with their career as well as with the company's resources. You need to show how you thought through the dilemma and made a good judgment. Good leaders will toss company policy out the window if it's stopping them from achieving their objectives.*

27

Please, take a seat

Delivering great answers to the interviewer's questions is the main skill in impressing people and getting the job; but let's not underestimate the importance of the body language you use to get yourself out there.

Neurolinguistic programming (NLP) can help you to develop rapport very quickly in an interview.

It includes techniques that can help you at the beginning of the interview when you're getting over your nerves and the interviewers are forming their first impression.

MATCHING AND MIRRORING

Interviews are like speed dating. You quickly eye each other up and decide whether or not you're interested in taking things further. So you need to be able to build rapport with your interviewer as quickly and effectively as possible. You never have a second chance to make a first impression.

The key skill to use here is mirroring. Mirroring body language is based on the theory that we are more at ease, subconsciously, with people who are similar to ourselves. It's a little like dancing. You can mirror most things.

Here's an idea for you...

It's probably best not to try the technique of mirroring for the first time in an interview. First of all, observe people doing it naturally at social gatherings. That gives you visual evidence that people do it, even in groups. Now try it in conversation with someone you know well, and then try it in a business context. Just a few practices should make you proficient enough to do it at an interview.

Posture, for instance. If they're upright, so are you. If they cross their legs, so do you. If their arms are on the table, so are yours. If you're sitting opposite someone with their right leg crossed, you cross your left leg to make a mirror image. You're making the person feel comfortable that they're talking to someone with similar behaviors to theirs.

Listen to the tone and speed of their voice. If they talk quickly, try to answer at the same speed. Vary your tone in the same way they do. Is the language they use concise or detailed? If they ask long questions they're going to be more comfortable with you giving a detailed answer.

Pick up on their mood, whether it's humorous or serious. You will notice, of course, how formally or casually they dress and conduct themselves.

You can mirror their use of gestures to accentuate a point. If they change their posture, you change yours. (People who are great at this technique claim to match the speed at which a person's eyes blink, but beginners shouldn't try this in case they look like a mole emerging into sunlight.)

Don't mimic them or copy their gestures too quickly. Mirroring is a subtle technique and interviewers who are not NLP proficient should not consciously notice what you're doing. They will just get the warm feeling that comes from dealing with someone on the same wavelength.

The importance of not boring panel members is discussed in IDEA 29, Talk me briefly through your history.

Try another idea...

We all use this form of body language when we're relaxed with our friends. Watch people in a restaurant or a pub and you'll see how mirroring helps the group to feel comfortable in each other's company. Or maybe it's the other way around: When you're with someone you're entirely comfortable with, it's quite hard not to do it.

ANCHORING

You're never at your most confident when you're about to be tested, professionally and personally. Anchoring can be very helpful in removing the signs of nervousness and helping to give you the confidence to do your best. Anchor yourself to a memory of a time in your life when you felt really confident. Before the interview, perhaps outside the door, pause and bring that experience of total confidence into your mind. Hold it there, remember how you felt and what you saw and said. This reminds your brain of how to feel and look confident. At times of pressure in the interview, recall the situation again and you'll adjust your behavior back to expressing confidence.

"She is the mirror of alle courteisye."
GEOFFREY CHAUCER

Defining idea...

How did it go?

Q   **I was mirroring an HR person in an interview. After ten minutes he made three really quick changes in the position of his arms and legs. I followed as slowly as I could. He then flung his arms back, stuck his legs right out until he was almost lying on the chair. I couldn't mirror this even if I'd wanted to, because I was wearing a skirt. What was going on?**

A   *We think he figured you out. Your movements were not subtle enough, or he was an expert in NLP and saw what you were doing. He was also probably teasing you; I suppose everyone has to have their fun and lots of HR folks don't get out that much. You did right to abandon your deliberate attempt to mirror his body language.*

Q   **I get terribly stressed out about interviews and never do myself justice. I tried anchoring and it worked really well at first. Then, halfway through the interview, someone else joined us and I started to feel really nervous. I didn't have time to think about the anchor again and the rest of the interview suffered as a result. Is it really possible to bring a happy time back into your mind in such circumstances?**

A   *Yes. Most interviewers will understand if you want to pause for breath. Generally, we're all too quick to reply to questions in this environment anyway. Practice taking pauses when you're in conversation. Pauses make you look thoughtful and pay an interviewer the compliment that their question was good enough to cause you to think. In those pauses you can recall your anchor. Try to control your breathing. If you get nervous you tend to talk from your throat rather than your diaphragm. Deep breathing will help with this and make you appear more confident.*

28

How does your present team see you?

Prepare for this one by thinking about yourself from other people's perspectives. Make sure you use examples to show, first, that you do know how people see you and, second, that you learn from their feedback.

Your prospective manager may use this sort of question to satisfy himself that you will fit into the team context he has planned for you.

Start with a positive point that you believe is a key strength in your ability to get the best out of people. It's wise to make this point using an unusual answer that doesn't seem to come straight out of the management books. Maybe, "Two members of the team have given me some interesting feedback. They thanked me for being very supportive of them inside our organization. I think it's my job to understand how the organization really works. This helps me to navigate internal politics and processes and so enable the team to get on with the work in an efficient and productive way."

Here's an idea for you... **Preparation for this is pretty straightforward. Make sure you have asked as many team members as you can what their perception of you is. If it is at all possible to tell them what you are doing, then do so. They will probably enjoy helping you to prepare for this question. Incidentally, the more open your relationship with your team is the better their contribution to your preparation will be. Make sure they always feel able to talk to you and give you feedback.**

STAY PEOPLE- NOT PROCESS-ORIENTED

It is probably best not to see this question as being about your management style. Nor is it appropriate to answer it with a short dissertation on objective- as opposed to task-based managers. Stay with your real impact on your people. The interviewers are looking for a high degree of self-insight here. "Although I know it's my job to explain the organization's strategy to my team, I also want them to be able to work without having to worry about that. They need to be able to rely on me to set objectives that reflect that strategy."

Think about why good people want to work for you. "They know I'm a net exporter of managers and team members to other parts of the organization." Most people want to work for a manager who will not stand in their way if there is an opportunity to make progress or to be promoted by moving jobs.

GOING WELL? TAKE A LITTLE RISK

If you feel that the interview is going well and that you have good rapport with the interviewer it's a good idea to show how you learn from either your mistakes or feedback from your team. (Much better to use feedback from your team as an example, rather than feedback from your boss.)

"I got quite a shock about eighteen months ago when a member of my team told me that I seemed to 'glaze over' when she talked about her personal situation. She said that I wasn't unhelpful and, indeed, that I asked her some good questions and even made some suggestions if she asked for them. It was just that I looked as though I didn't want to be involved in that particular conversation. Since then I have made sure that when such a discussion starts my body language and eye contact make it clear that I am interested and want to help."

The management style thing arises in IDEA 43, *What's your style of influencing people?*

Try another idea…

If you are at an internal interview the chances are that the interviewer will have talked to one or two members of your team. They will also have heard your peer team leaders discussing your strengths and weaknesses. So don't overstate any perception that you want your team to have of you if there's any chance that it might have been contradicted. Look for hints of this when supplementary questions come in such as, "Do they think that you have enough influence in getting a senior manager to change something if it would help them?" Don't duck it; at least tell them you are working on that area of the team leader's job.

How did it go?

Q   **The annual appraisal system in my organization includes a section on how my people see me and so on. That's enough, isn't it? Surely we don't want to encourage people to give their opinions all the time, do we?**

A   *Well, yes, actually. It is widely accepted now that an open management style is more effective than what used to be called the "mushroom style." (Keep them in the dark and throw a bucket of manure over them from time to time.) If you do it your way, you're making people bottle up the problems they've got for a once-a-year opportunity to talk about them.*

Q   **Are you seriously suggesting that I ask junior members of my team what they think of my performance, despite the fact that they know nothing about our business and less about how to manage a team?**

A   *Yes. It's astonishing what you can learn from such people. They can have terrific insights into the business because they're still looking at the wood, not the trees. For personal insights, who better to ask than someone who has only recently formed their early impression of you? If we were you, we'd not only ask the most junior people for feedback but we'd tell an interviewer what we'd done and what we'd learned from their reply.*

29

Talk me briefly through your history

A relatively easy one if you've done your preparation work well. The only real risk is that you'll talk about the wrong thing, so keep checking that what you're saying is relevant.

You can't play this one by ear; or if you do you're taking a huge risk. It's crucial to have prepared a few sentences about each aspect of your history that they'll be interested in.

The question cries out for clarifying questions in return. "Is there any particular aspect of my previous experience that you want me to talk about?" This is a fair question and means that you're focusing on what they're truly interested in. It may be wise to tell them something before you ask the question; but don't go on too long without trying to find out exactly what they're looking for.

AND THIS ENABLED ME TO...

The main secret to a blistering answer to this one is to take an aspect of your working life, tell them about it, and end each story with what you learned from the

Get a focus into this answer that aims at the heart of the job by preparing two stories in each of the three areas of investigation: personal attributes or leadership qualities, technical/functional capabilities, ambition and future aspirations. Make sure that all the stories end up relevant to some aspect of the job description. If you get it right and all the stories fit with what they're looking for, you're starting to look uniquely like the person they had in mind.

experience. And make sure that what you learned hits a hot button in the description of the job you're applying for. Here are some examples that show how the learning experience fits with the profile of the person they're looking for:

"College was a big step for me. I learned how to learn, and also how to stand on my own two feet. Suddenly, there was no one interested in whether I was doing the work except me. It obviously helped me become self-motivating. Since I was a History major, I had to write a lot of essays. This has proved very useful. I use those researching and writing skills to produce reports in my current job."

"After two years as a junior sales manager I was invited to take on a two-year assignment in the sales training and development department. This gave me three main things. First, I became an expert in all aspects of the theory of selling. Second, I became a very experienced presenter and coach, helping everyone from rookies to seasoned professionals learn new skills. I also pushed into new areas like remote learning and using technology in training. Finally, it gave me experience in talking to just about every division in the business. This last part gave me good exposure to the board and I formed a good idea of what happens at that level in the business."

"I spent an interesting year as the project controller of a big IT project. This involved keeping the project control system up to date, charting progress, and spotting early-warning signs that events or activities were running late. I learned a huge amount about complex project management by working very closely with the project manager."

For more about using your leisure time to sell yourself take a look at IDEA 16, *My hobbies are Ping-Pong, playing the ukulele, and going to the theater.*

Try another idea...

Check also as you go along that you're covering the right level of detail by asking clarifying questions. "Is this what you're looking for?" "Do you want me to give more detail in this area, or have you got what you want?"

GO A BIT PERSONAL, TOO

It's always good in a brief history of you to mention some aspect of how you spend your leisure time. Leave it until the end and try to get a little humor into it. Make sure that even though it's your leisure you're talking about, it still has relevance to the job you're applying for: "I also coach Little League. I enjoy coaching very much. Believe me, you learn a lot about motivation technique, particularly when you're encouraging the team to play better and enjoy the seventh inning when it's already twenty-nine to zero."

"What history and experience teach us is this—that nations and governments have never learnt anything from history, or acted upon any lessons they might have drawn from it."
G. W. F. HEGEL

Defining idea...

How did it go? **Q** **I did the analysis of the job description that you suggested. It seemed to major on teamwork. So I made two of my longest stories illustrate my experience and skills in working as a team member. I even used a sports example for my personal story. I was somewhat taken aback when one of the interviewers asked if I realized that I would essentially be working on my own for much of the time. Don't you think I would've done better to concentrate on demonstrating self-motivation or something like that?**

A *You could have found a way to recover by picking another story that shows how well you did with a job alone and without a leader. Incidentally, did you check the relevance of the first story before going on to the second? If you did, that could have revealed the inconsistency earlier.*

Q **It was taking awhile for me to get to the most important part of my career in terms of doing this job when the interviewer said that we should move on to another question. What do you make of that?**

A *Maybe you should have gotten to the main point quicker. In our experience, people do tend to go on rather long, particularly about their early days. Anyway, keep the main point in your head and use it as the answer to another question.*

30

How do you manage projects?

At some point you're going to have a somewhat technical discussion about the nitty-gritty of the job you're applying for. Make sure you get the details right for the audience you're speaking to.

Interviewers want to hire interesting people who can steer clear of jargon when required and display a personality that will contribute to the atmosphere of the workplace. They don't want to hire complete bores.

It's quite possible that someone, probably the potential manager, will want to have a detailed technical discussion with you. If it's a one-on-one then that's fine. Go with the flow and enjoy talking to a fellow enthusiast. We're using this example to point out the pitfalls of such a discussion when other people—HR maybe, or a senior manager—are also present.

Here's an idea for you... **Figure out how to explain your job to a layperson in 100 words. Remember you've got to explain it in a way that shows that you have a wealth of knowledge and experience that makes you a reliable resource to get the job done. Done that? OK, try it out on a few people. Teenagers are a good bet, since you can measure their concentration span in nanoseconds. When you've made that work, reduce it to fifty words.**

FIND THE CONNECTION

You've got to say enough, of course, to prove that you have the technical ability to do the job. But leave any detail about that until after you've presented the answer in a way that shows the bridge between what your function is and how the organization succeeds. We'll use the project management question to illustrate this idea, but it works for any function.

A project, or any department or function, has its internal issues. You have to get the team to carry out the function and meet its objectives. But what outside managers are interested in is the interface where the project contributes to or harms the success of the organization. They're also interested in the project when it has an impact on other parts of the organization. These are the bridges you're looking for when it comes to describing to nontechnical people how you'll go about the job. In selling terms you're looking for the "benefits" your function brings to the party.

So, "At the outset, I develop the objectives of the project and spend whatever time it takes to get all the stakeholders' agreement that we've got them right" is much better than, "While not a perfect critical path analysis engine, Microsoft Project can be used to control the project and it has the benefit that most people are used to using it."

Similarly, "I'd talk to as many managers with relevant experience as possible to work out the resources we'd need during the project" is much better than, "Once you've got the action plan, the resource plan is quite straightforward. All you have to do is to reproduce the action plan as a resource plan."

There's a link here with another question to which you could give a too-long reply. It's in IDEA 42, *Tell me about yourself.*

Try another idea...

KEEP IT VERY, VERY SIMPLE

The lurking snake in this type of question is the fact that you're probably going straight into your comfort zone. You've got the qualifications to do the job, you've had the training to do the job, and you've got experience of doing the job; so it's a whole lot easier to spend time on this part than on tricky questions about subjects such as managing difficult people or making sure the customer drives your strategic plan. So we go on and on and on.

There's another useful technique here to keep things simple. Give them the simplest possible explanation of how you manage a project. Then ask them if they want more detail. In this example it could be as simple as, "Planning a project needs forward thinking: Who and what do I need to get the job done? It also needs backward thinking: If it's got to be finished by the end of the year what needs to be done and when?"

"A healthy male adult bore consumes each year one and a half times his weight in other people's patience."
JOHN UPDIKE, novelist

Defining idea...

How did
it go?

Q   **I know exactly what you mean with this one. But what you're suggesting doesn't work! I had a very difficult time in my last interview with a technical person and her boss's boss. I tried to give "bridge" type answers but every time she brought me back to the detail of what I did in my last job and what I would do if offered this job. I could see that the senior guy was losing interest: He was starting to read a report he'd taken out of his briefcase. How could I have stopped this?**

A   *You've got to confront the problem here. Ask a question of the senior person like, "Am I going into too much detail for you?" They may say, "No, no, go on." In which case you do. Or they may decide to move on. Remember that all your competitors will have had the same problem and some will have happily gone into huge detail and completely turned the senior person off.*

Q   **It's not possible to digest my complex job into a hundred words, let alone fifty. What am I supposed to do?**

A   *Don't forget that politicians and generals only need the answer to six questions—such as, "Do we have enough fuel to carry out the campaign?"—in order to decide whether to go to war or not.*

31

How ambitious are you?

How do you explain that your career path is shaped like a bullet but that you realize you have to get your head down and do this job well? Be honest and enthusiastic but mainly be eager to prove yourself in the job you're applying for.

The key person here is the most senior person involved in interviewing you. They're the ones looking for talent to join their organization, not just someone to do a job.

This question has many guises. Here are a few: "Where do you see yourself in five years' time?" "In an ideal world what job would eventually fulfill your dreams?" And even, "When do you expect a promotion?"

THE SKY'S THE LIMIT

Start from an honest and reasonable answer to the question. "Well, I certainly want to move forward and have a career that makes good progress. I know that my career will depend first and foremost on doing well in the job I go into. As I do that job I'll also become a more knowledgeable professional in this organization and in this

"Where do you want to be in five years' time?" is not a bad question to ask yourself. If you have a clear career path in your head you'll handle questions like this better. Supposing that each job will last for a minimum of eighteen months and probably more like two years, the question prompts you to ask yourself about the next two moves after this job. With such a thought in your head you're well equipped to check the feasibility of this plan during the interview.

industry. This will allow me to focus my energies and skills in the areas that are key to the success of the company. I think it'll take a couple of years to get into that position and at that point I'll have a much more informed view of what is possible. But my starting point is that I'm looking to get ahead."

The key is to show that you are ambitious but not arrogant enough to know exactly where you want to be. There are some uncertainties, not the least of which is that as yet you don't really know where the key jobs in the organization lie. This makes a good finish to your answer: "What do you think over the next few years will be the crucial areas for your organization to exploit?" There's not a lot else you can say here, but it's an excellent opportunity to ask questions and get them to talk about prospects in their company in general and your prospects in particular.

DON'T LOOK MORE INTERESTED THAN THE JOB JUSTIFIES

Sometimes this question is asked for the opposite reason. Some jobs, particularly in small organizations, don't offer an obvious career path or opportunities for advancement. Here's an example:

A small training company offers a course to qualified lawyers to keep their legal knowledge up to date. The lecturers are all lawyers. They are looking for a receptionist/administrator to help prepare the rooms, welcome clients as they arrive for the course, and provide the refreshment at breaks and lunchtime. Apart from getting more involved in preparing visual aids and handouts, there is no real career progression. Who're they going to take on for the job? They don't want a complete deadbeat, someone who will settle for the job for life. Such a person won't do a good job with the clients if they just feel that their job is to make the coffee. But the company has nothing further to offer. If a job like this suits you for a period of time then go for it and tell them just that. "I want to get into a more senior job, perhaps in a firm partnership. This job is ideal for me to learn about the people and the profession, particularly because I'll meet a lot of different people from different firms. I'm happy to spend, say, a couple of years doing this and then if I have to move on to get ahead I'll consider doing so. Is that a sensible plan?" Finishing with the question puts the whole issue on the table. Either you've got it dead right or they're looking for a complete deadbeat.

Another good career-oriented question is IDEA 41, What gets you up in the morning?

Try another idea...

"Ambitious young people should be reasonably patient and hold the success of the company as more important than their own success."
JOHN EGAN, executive

Defining idea...

"You cannot leave you career development solely to your employer—he just is not good enough to manage this for you!"
NEVILLE BAIN, executive

Defining idea...

143

How did it go?

Q   **I had a long conversation on this topic with my potential boss and a more senior manager who seemed very interested in me. It became clear that the former didn't like my talking about the future; he kept coming back for reassurance that I wanted to do the job we were discussing. I felt a bit torn. What should I have done?**

A   *Probably pretty much what you did. Continue the conversation about the future with the senior person and keep reassuring the manager. It sounds as though the senior person has plans in mind for you, so go with it. If, and it seems unlikely, the manager goes against you because of your ambition, their boss will probably find you something else.*

Q   **My ambition is actually to come out of business at an appropriate time and go into politics full-time. I think a future manager would be impressed by that ambition. Do you think I should tell them?**

A   *Not if you want to get the job. Everyone thinks, and they're probably right, that aspiring politicians dedicate a huge part of their lives to getting elected, doing party business, and so on. Rightly or wrongly, potential employers are going to think that you will give the job second place.*

32

Why do you want to work for this company?

Time to put on display the huge amount of research you did to get ready for this interview.

All interviewees know a lot about themselves and their aspirations. Only a few have the competitive edge of knowing a lot about the organization and its aspirations.

There are now so many sources of information about businesses that you should be able to do a thorough analysis in a fairly short period of time.

WHAT DO YOU NEED TO KNOW?

Here are the headings:
- industry sector
- aims and strategy
- company/divisional structure
- financial performance last year
- main customers and competitors
- products and people

Here's an idea for you...

To prepare more deeply for this question you can use SWOT analysis of their situation. Take the mission statement or aims and objectives you got from the report and ask the question, "In terms of achieving that objective what are the company's Strengths, Weaknesses, Opportunities, and Threats?" This will give you good ammunition for demonstrating knowledge and some good questions to ask about the company and its plans.

Find the website of someone who analyzes this industry sector. That will give you a good overview and identify the organization's place in the scheme of things. Then phone the company and ask for a hard copy of their annual report—they're used to being asked for them. The hard copy is better than the web version because you can see how glossy the report is, or how thrifty, or how environmentally friendly—all good clues. You'll discover the aims and strategy in the chairman's statement and the chief executive's report. The structure will be clear from the divisional reports that follow in the report. Note the overall structure and then read carefully about the part you're trying to join. It's only high level, but that's exactly what you need to answer this question.

There's a summary of the organization's financial performance in the chairman's and finance director's statements. It would be good to be able to say, "Your profitability is still growing well, compared both with last year and with the rest of the industry." If you're going for a finance job, of course, you'll need to do all the financial ratios.

Most annual reports talk about the main customers they're proud of. It's good to have a success story from among these to talk about: "You certainly did no harm to your reputation when Powergen spoke about the Dallas project."

It's easy enough to find out about the company's products and services. You need to know the whole breadth of what they do. It's good if you can find out something about their reputation for treating their people. This helps you to know whether you want to work for them and gives you a nice compliment to pay them during the interview.

We look at this question from a job/person fit in IDEA 33, *So, why do you want this job?*

Try another idea...

We recommend you look at two of their competitors, either by obtaining their annual reports or by visiting their websites. If you can experience the company from a customer's point of view—for example, in retail—then you should certainly do so.

RELATE YOUR KNOWLEDGE OF THE COMPANY TO THE JOB

Start with the sector: "You're in the gas sector, which is still a pretty exciting place to be. The market's growing and companies in the industry are still jockeying for position in the new competitive environment." Now move on to the company. It's great to start with a quote: "Your chairman said, 'The group's excellent performance has been combined with major progress in the establishment of a culture that seeks continual operational improvements, high service standards, and, above all, safety.' These are all values I share and, since I'm applying for the job of safety supervisor in Sector 7G, I particularly like the emphasis on safety. The financial strength is attractive, too; I want to work somewhere that can afford to keep up with the huge amounts of capital investment you need to put in just to stand still—plus some for innovation. According to

"For also knowledge itself is power."
FRANCIS BACON

Defining idea...

147

the Gas Producers Council, a lot of investment still needs to go into offshore safety, for example."

Keep the answer to the company itself; don't go into the attraction of the job unless they ask you to do that. You're trying to keep yourself out of this reply and concentrate on something you know they're vitally interested in—their own company.

Finally, ask a question to get them talking about the same thing: "I wasn't sure from what I could read about you whether your ventures abroad are likely to expand or not. Can you tell me that?"

Q **That's fine for a big public company. But I'm going to see a little training company that hasn't posted its last year's accounts online. How do I do all this for them?**

How did it go?

A *You'll have to come clean and ask them for anything they can give you: brochures, company profiles, newspaper articles, and so on. You can still research their industry. How do little players fare? Who are the big boys they'll be competing against? Would it be possible to talk to one of their customers? The latter are a great source of information and often happy to talk about their experience. It'll knock the interviewer's socks off if you give them feedback they were unaware of from a customer. If you can't get what you need by research, make a note and ask about it at the interview.*

Q **I used this stuff and it went over really well. The only time I stumbled was when I said something that was out-of-date. We talked at cross-purposes for a while until they understood what had gone wrong. Anything I could have done to avoid that?**

A *They're the experts and they're bound to know much more than is published. You ought to check their website or the site of a financial newspaper to get the most recent information about them.*

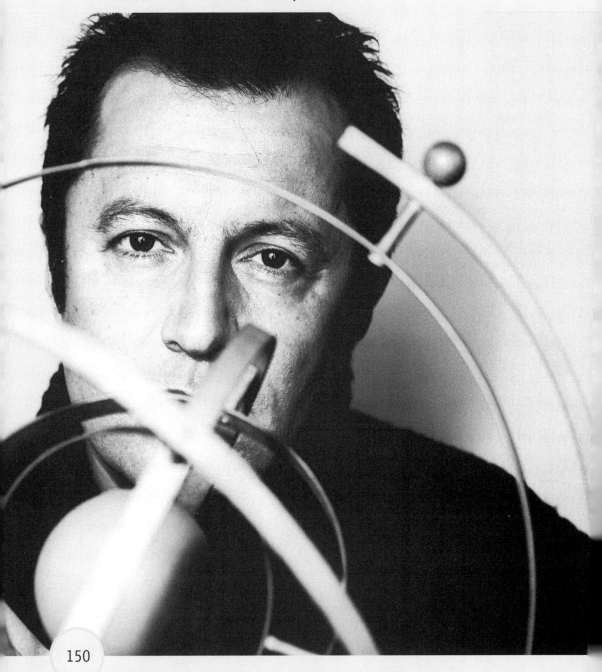

33

So, why do you want this job?

Turn a question like this into a selling opportunity by using a double answer—balance what you'll get out of the job with what they'll get out of hiring you.

It should be reasonably easy to answer this one as long as you're going for the right job. If it's very difficult, then ask yourself if this is the right employer for you before you go in.

An employer wants people to join them with enthusiasm for the challenges they're about to face. Similarly, you want to get into an environment where your working life gives you joy rather than grief. Research and good self-insight will give you the right answer to achieve both aims.

WHAT'S IN IT FOR ME?

It's probably best to start the dual answer with the straightforward answer. It's another question that depends on your research. You've got to be able to reply in terms of the company's attributes as you find them. It doesn't really matter what the situation is; you can still paint it as ideal for you. "Most people want to work for the market leader; I could use your name with pride" could equally be, "I like the

Here's an idea for you...

This question really is one to prepare for carefully. The time will never be wasted, since this question will always crop up in one way or other. The best way to prepare is to find someone to play the interviewer and then try out with them the actual words you're going to use. If you can get someone in the same industry that would be best, but anyone with good experience in organizations or business should be able to help.

way you've made such progress in your industry over the last few years. A growing company like yours suits my energetic way of working. I really enjoy success."

Now try to get in something about their reputation. "I understand that you can offer me a stable, challenging, and inspiring work environment—you certainly have that reputation. I think it's the sort of environment that brings out the best in me."

Now compliment the company on what it actually does. "Many people regard your products and services as the best around. It's a pride thing again; I like to work for someone who is passionate about service and quality. I think we share those values and that I would enjoy fitting into your team."

AND WHAT'S IN IT FOR THEM?

Your unique selling proposition is you and your skills and experience. Try to figure out a way of illustrating that everything you've done points at you being the right person for them. Perhaps start from specific experience. For a team leader in credit control: "My experience in the credit control department of a builders' union was, frankly, a hard school. The building industry is always suffering from companies going under. I know about collection periods, credit ratings calculated from company reports, and, of course, I've heard every excuse under the sun for not being quite ready to issue the check. I think that as team leader I would be able to help others to learn from that experience."

Now relate the specific skills to the goals of the organization. "I understand the benefits to you of getting payment in on time or even before time because I've controlled cash flow for an organization and seen the impact it can have on profitability."

You can also be more open about your skills where you're sure they're appropriate. For a production manager: "I've always scored well in problem solving and from what you've said you need to find some new ways of cutting down the waste at the end of the production line."

Something more personal can emphasize your uniqueness. For a training manager: "The fact that I've done a bit of amateur theater helps me to understand the 'performance' side of running a training course."

Now bring the three things together: "So you see why I was excited when I saw your job ad; you seem to need a person with pretty much the experience, skills, and interests that I've developed."

If the job you're going for involves a degree of creativity you could use IDEA 39, *Tell me about a time you generated a creative solution to a problem*, to give you some more ammunition.

Try another idea...

"And so my fellow Americans: ask not what your country can do for you—ask what you can do for your country."
JOHN F. KENNEDY

Defining idea...

How did it go?

Q I've thought long and hard about this. There's a good job in a company that's not doing very well. I think part of the problem is that they don't focus on teamwork. They have a reputation for "hire and fire" and come off as a little "every man for himself." When they ask this question should I point out that while I'm not sure I share their current values I think I can introduce some new ones that will help to improve their performance?

A *Possibly. Our first reaction to this was "NO. Wait until you've got the job and then sell the changes that you think they need to make." But on second thought you could be right. Depends if you think that someone in the room is thinking the same way as you, in which case go for it. You could get the pleasant surprise of one of them telling you that they know they need to change in this area—in which case your preparation is ideal. (Sorry to be skeptical, but you should also bear in mind the words in script font on page 151.)*

Q I'd like to end this answer with a bold statement. Can I say that I would like to be in my boss's position within two years—in order to demonstrate my ambition?

A *Yes, but choose the words carefully. You're trying to make them feel confident about you, not insecure. Try, "Finally, I have aspirations to get to your level in the not too distant future."*

34

How easy are you to work with?

This is the real question hidden under a number of aliases. In this part of the interview they're probing for how you work with your boss and whether you are likely to be an employee who causes problems rather than one who resolves them.

You've got to show loyalty, stability, and that you will be an easy person to work with and manage.

Such a question may come toward the end of an interview when they've been watching your performance for half an hour or more. Their concern is that it is a "performance" and they want to make sure that they understand the real you.

WHO IS THE REAL YOU?

They can ask this question in various guises. "How do you get along with your current boss?" What they're looking for here is any sign that you will rock the boat in their department. One of the most disruptive things you can get in an

Here's an idea for you...

Think about a colleague or friend whom you know to have been critical of and disloyal to their boss. What did they say? It might have been very open or it might have been more surreptitious. Now think about the impact that had on their team. Were they sucked into the same opinion and did they also start to express it? Did it contribute to or hinder the team's performance? This brings home the characteristics and behavior of a person who finds it difficult to play in a team, and their potential impact.

organization is a person who sows seeds of doubt about the competence or character of the manager or team leader. So it's a straightforward, "Personally, we get on well: He's easy to work for and I think we have achieved quite a lot together." Try to say no more, although it's likely that they'll ask supplementary questions to get you to substantiate what you've just said. They could go close to the bone with, "I've heard that he doesn't consult much when he's making a decision." Just stay with a positive attitude: "I haven't found that." There's little possibility that they're actually interested in the character or competence of your boss; they're just probing to see if they can get you to display disloyalty.

"How are you on taking instructions?" An easy-to-manage person is one who likes to be given objectives and tasks that are well explained at the outset. Then they just get on with it and deliver. But they're also aware that circumstances do arise where a team leader may at short notice take them off their current task and ask them to do something else. With this question the interviewers are checking that you're a team player and that you recognize that, from time to time, your boss will give you brief directions and expect compliance. You can probably find a dual answer that covers both points. "I like to work in an environment where the logic behind what I'm being asked to do is clear. But I understand that I won't know about all the pressures and deadlines that exist. This may very well mean that I have to do something without knowing all the details leading up to the directions I've been given. This is fine by me because it's just a part of working in a fast-moving, competitive environment."

They want to know how well you'll fit into the culture of a company; so try IDEA 43, What's your style of influencing people?

Try another idea...

WORKING UNDER STRESS

"What keeps you awake at night?" This is not a therapist's question aimed at finding out your innermost fears; it's an attempt to get to know your ability to handle stress. So answer it from a professional point of view: Take it as entirely business related. "I'm concerned by the normal things a sales manager worries about: meeting targets, eking out the budget, avoiding heavy discounting, and so on. But I've handled these issues for a while and I certainly don't let them get me down."

"Some people think that the business term FIFO stands for First In First Out; but in this organization it stands for Fit In or F*@! Off."
Speaker protected under the Fifth Amendment of the Constitution

Defining idea...

How did it go?

Q **I thought long and hard about this because, according to your line of logic, I displayed some very disloyal behavior when I first joined an organization. When I arrived, my boss was also quite new and a number of the older members of his team were very critical of him, comparing him very unfavorably with his predecessor. It was easy to join in and I did. The trouble is that they were right and he didn't last long. If I'd gone for an interview at the time I was working for him, should I have shown complete loyalty as you suggest or indicated that I knew what his shortcomings were? After all, not everybody's perfect and the interviewer knows it.**

A *Think about it from the interviewers' point of view. Your organization, in its wisdom, put that guy in charge. If they think their wisdom got it wrong and they change things, that's up to them. Your job was to help your boss, whatever he was like, to succeed. It's certainly not anyone's job to undermine him and make his failure more certain.*

Q **This stress thing. Don't you think you've gone a bit far? Surely an interviewer wants to believe that you feel something for the company as well as work for it. Surely not being able to sleep at night from time to time is a demonstration of that.**

A *Look, we're not saying it never happens; but it really shouldn't. If you have a problem at work, the company has the same problem. They want you to come in the next morning refreshed and ready to hug the monster. You can't do that if you've spent the whole night rattling your worry beads.*

35

What is the one thing your team would most like to change about you?

Knowing yourself, or self-insight, is crucial. The answer to this question tells the interviewers a lot about you, probably including a hint of your main weakness.

Pick the thing to be changed carefully—and turn a vice into a virtue.

Let's look first at the negative side. What they are probing for here is any trait of yours that really is a red light for them not to go ahead with you. So avoid showing them any problem that might be a deal breaker.

USE ANCIENT HISTORY

A neat way of handling this is to talk about a weakness that you've had in the past that you've overcome but remain on guard for. "A manager once pointed out to me that I was causing some discomfort to my team when I acted too precipitately when they came to me with a problem. I thought about it and realized that I sometimes listened to a problem and quickly proposed a solution. I might then

Here's an idea for you...

Prepare for this type of question by actually asking it of your team. "What would you most like to change about me?" With luck what they say won't be a surprise and you can figure out an answer using the templates in this Idea. Perhaps it will be a surprise, in which case you've just taken a big step forward in getting to know yourself.

volunteer to take the first action myself. At that point I'd pick up the phone there and then to put the action plan into progress. I talked to the team about it and they agreed that it was frustrating for them because they wanted to go away, think about the plan, and figure out the problem themselves. I think I've fixed it and don't do it now; but I'm aware of the tendency and watch myself carefully in those circumstances."

This is a reasonable answer and one that shows your ability to act on criticism. Which is pertinent to another question in the area of self-insight which often comes up: "How do you react when your manager or a team member tells you that they don't like something you do?" Now, nobody's perfect and such criticism happens to everyone. It's crucial that you display real interest in the feedback and take some action to show that you are putting things right. There's no need, however, to suggest to an interviewer that such things happen very often.

"I've come to know that whatever the criticism that people are making, there is always something in it; so I never argue about it or attempt to justify my position. In order to learn from it, I've found that you need to talk it over thoroughly, to make sure that you're both talking about exactly the same thing. When I do that, it's normally pretty easy to modify how I behave. If I then invite them to point out any reoccurrences I find that the discussion ends up useful and amicable."

PICK SOMETHING THEY ACTUALLY LIKE

This depends on your function. Every job has a part that people don't like or see as a low priority. For a salesperson it's easy. No one likes doing the paperwork. Often in a rather macho way, people regard it as getting in the way of the real work—the selling work. Once again, present the issue as something you know you have to continuously overcome.

There's another self-insight question in IDEA 46, *Is your glass half-empty or half-full?*

Try another idea...

"I know I have a tendency to get a bit behind with the paperwork. I also know that that can upset the office people and, if left undone for long enough, can lead to missed deliveries and customer dissatisfaction. So, I've disciplined myself to keep paperwork up to date every Wednesday afternoon when a lot of my customers are closed." Whatever your function you can probably find your version of the salesperson's paperwork.

"The real solvent of class distinction is a proper measure of self-esteem—a kind of unconsciousness. Some people are at ease with themselves, so the world is at ease with them."
ALAN BENNETT, British playwright

Defining idea...

How did it go?

Q **Oh my goodness, I did it! I talked to the team and they completely threw me. They accused me of being too quick to show frustration and even anger when I thought that someone had made a mistake or wasn't pulling their weight. I honestly thought that I was just raising my voice to make a point. Not only that, but I'm going for an internal promotion; so the interviewer may have had this feedback. What can I do?**

A *We did warn you that you might get a big step forward in self-knowledge. In the circumstances, you should probably expect a question along the lines of this Idea and choose that weakness as your example. You should be able to find an example that employs the "use ancient history" method and shows that you know about the problem and that you're working on it. You could also try to turn this shock into a positive by telling the interviewer that you talked to the team as part of your preparation. "They made me aware that I have to continue working on maintaining a positive attitude at all times, especially to under-performers."*

Q **I'm a saleswoman and used the "I'm sometimes bad at the paperwork" line. I said it quite wittily and the sales manager laughed. The HR person then grilled me about it and asked me if I understood that letting the admin slip can cause real problems. By the end of that, I don't think I'd done myself any favors. Don't you agree?**

A *It looks as though your answer was right on for the sales manager. But, since there was someone else there it would have been wiser to take a more sober approach. Perhaps make the witty remark, then quickly go on to demonstrate that you really do understand the problems created by poor paperwork.*

36

Do you enjoy hard work?

It's a lousy question, so hit it out of the park. What do they expect you to say? "Good Lord, no, I've always tried to keep my head down and avoid the real action."

If what they mean by "hard work" is energy and drive, then, yes, you've got it in spades.

This is a closed question, but the answer "yes" won't be enough. You'll be surprised how easy it is to take a closed question like this and mold it into some points that you want to make in almost any area you care to choose. So it's an opportunity to deliver the set pieces that you have so carefully prepared. You could go toward the "work/life balance" or "don't work harder; work smarter" or anything that shows you will be an energetic contributor to their enterprise. We'll look at the question as it is and then at other questions getting at the same thing.

YOU CAN ALWAYS MAKE THINGS BETTER

"I've always been enthusiastic about my work. I've generally been in jobs that I enjoy, so that makes putting the effort in really easy. This is particularly true when I'm working for an organization with whose objectives I can easily identify." You can try balancing an answer like that with another benefit they're after—people who are constantly looking for ways that they and their team can do things better.

Here's an idea for you...

Find a good example of when you've looked at your or a team member's work and found a really effective procedural change that you got the company to accept. What was the benefit to the organization of making that change? What was the benefit to the individual? Such an example is sure to come in useful for this type of question or another.

"I do regard it as part of everyone's job to suggest improvements. When I've asked people in my team if they can see better ways that they could use to get the job done, it's amazing; in almost every case the answer is yes. This is also true if you ask them about their interface with other parts of the organization. They can always suggest even very small changes that another department could make that would make their job easier and their performance more effective. So if I or other people in the team are having to work longer and longer hours, it's always worth looking for suggestions as to how we can improve the way the work gets done."

This could lead to, "How would you deal with a person in your team who complained continuously about how hard they had to work?" To which you might reply, "First of all I'd take it very seriously. I'd ask them to discuss it with me and perhaps keep a record of their activities over a period of time. We'd look together for ways to reduce their workload or change our systems and procedures in some way. If I became sure that we were making unreasonable demands on the person, I'd raise the matter with my boss and try to find a solution. You have to be careful, though. I've found that some people do work hard, but don't want to change anything—not even the fact that they moan all the time about how hard they have to work."

OTHER PROBES IN THIS AREA

IDEA 51, *How do you get things done?*, is a related question in this area.

Try another idea...

"How are you at working under pressure?" To which you might say, "Oh, I've had to handle that in all my jobs and I'm comfortable in that environment. Having said that, I try to plan ahead and avoid deadlines and crises creeping up on the team or me. That way we keep the pressure at a reasonable level."

"Are you most comfortable with fairly regular hours?" Answer this one as usual with a balance: "I'm well aware that in a competitive industry such as this you can't expect to work completely regular hours. In fact, I'm not sure I'd like to have to do that. But there are some regular parts of my family life that I like to protect. For example, last year my daughter went to ballet every Wednesday evening. It suited us for me to take her and her friend to the class. I therefore agreed with my boss that I would always get away on time on a Wednesday and it worked out well."

"Work expands so as to fill the time available for its completion."
C. NORTHCOTE PARKINSON, British historian

Defining idea...

165

How did it go?

Q **I tried your advice on this one and I think it made me look work shy. I explained how we'd found a way around some work that a colleague was doing—which gave her much more spare time. The guy in the interview said that it sounded as if she and I were just looking for shortcuts. Did I make a mistake in the way I presented this?**

A *Well done; shortcuts are exactly what we should all be looking for as long as they don't compromise quality. Perhaps the mistake you made is in the wording "spare time." Could you have explained what she was able to get done in that "spare time," like finding new customers or working on the administration backlog? But we think it's bad luck to meet someone who thinks the word "shortcut" is pejorative.*

Q **I really liked the idea of setting one day a week when I had to get away on time, and went to my boss to negotiate Tuesdays. She said that I was being unreasonable and that she couldn't give me any such guarantee. She told me that we were in business to make a profit and that meant being open when people wanted to buy. Why didn't this request work?**

A *We wonder if you were clear enough about why Tuesday was so important to you. And did you try to see it from her point of view before making the request? It would have been good if you could have proposed how it would always be feasible to cover for you on those evenings.*

37

Do you feel your lack of financial knowledge will be a disadvantage?

You won't check every box on their wish list, so you need to know the key ones. Think through what you think they will regard as essential attributes and use the interview to check them out.

Good interviewers will cover a broad range of topics. Researching or second-guessing the key ones helps you to hit the hot buttons and skate elegantly over the thinner ice.

Most companies, and probably all large companies, are well organized when they go recruiting. Their managers will have done their preparation aided by HR contacts and processes. They've agreed to talk to you, so it's unlikely that your resumé has revealed a deal breaker. You'll have some knowledge of how important, say, financial knowledge is to this job from reading the job posting carefully and asking for the job description before you go to the interview.

Make sure you're applying for the right jobs. If the same lack of knowledge or experience keeps stopping you from getting jobs, you'll have to do something radical about it or work out an alternative route to getting where you want to be. It's never a good idea to keep banging your head against a brick wall. The best people to help you understand the real problem are those who've interviewed you and not selected you. Ask all of them for feedback in the specific area where they felt your knowledge and experience let you down. Talk to them about whether and how you could fix it.

IF THEY CAN DO IT, YOU CAN DO IT

First of all, know where the thin ice is. The chances are you already know where your weak areas lie for this job. But if you're uncertain what their priorities might be, use their own system to figure it out. Make a table with three columns. In the left-hand column put down the knowledge and experience you think they will be looking for. Some will be straightforward, such as "project management"; others softer, like "motivating third parties." Now anticipate their weighing the importance of each of the capabilities you've identified, using a scale of 1–10, and write these in the second column. In the third column use a scale of 1–10 to record candidly your position right now. The best thing to do next is to check your opinion with someone who knows you and your work well. Now you should know what questions may be raised. How should you answer them?

TURNING A VICE INTO A VIRTUE

First, admit the weakness and show enthusiasm about fixing it. "Yes, I know that's a little bit of a chink in my armor, but it's one I want to fix and this job is a great opportunity to do that. My view is that I can do that in time to avoid any risk to achieving the goals of the job." Their response to this will give you some clues as to whether there's a real problem or not. If they say, "Yes, you're right," you've not only answered the question but removed the obstacle. In any case, make sure your answer exhibits "good self-insight" here. At least you know your weaknesses.

For a breakdown of leadership capabilities use IDEA 26, *What makes you a good leader?*

Try another idea...

Another way of handling this is to say that in the past you've found that often a new person in a team who does lack experience in one particular area may actually come up with a new angle that the team, used to operating in their usual way, might have missed.

Incidentally, if your weakness is in an area such as finance—a weakness mainly of knowledge—take heart. It's a lot easier to pick up such knowledge from a book than to earn the trust of your team or to manage difficult people. Point that out in the nicest possible way.

If they're still showing some concern it's a good idea to have already done something about the weak area. In this particular instance try, "I knew that finance was a weak area so I took some advice from a financial controller on

"He had read Shakespeare and found him weak in chemistry."
H. G. WELLS

Defining idea...

which book I should read. She suggested *Smart Things to Know about Business Finance* by Ken Langdon and Alan Bonham; so I bought it and am currently reading it."

Another useful technique here is the parallel answer—"I haven't done that, but I have done this":

Them: "Tell me about your experience in mergers and acquisitions."
You: "I haven't been directly involved with M&A, but I have handled complex projects where I had to rely on outside people for their particular expertise."

How did it go?

Q **OK, I did the table and found it quite helpful. There is, however, one area where I think they're looking for an 8 on the scale and I'm probably a 4. Should I try to ignore this finding at the interview?**

A *Everyone's different, but we'd suggest you might bring this issue up early in the discussion. If you try to ignore it you might look nervous or not do yourself justice because you're sitting there hoping the topic will not be raised. Secondly, it's more impressive for you to have realized that you have this deficiency, and be prepared to do something about it, than to be found out by an awkward question.*

Q **There's a technical area in the job I'm applying for that they'll think is important but I happen to know is actually old hat and easily gotten around in other ways. What if I can't persuade them that they're out-of-date?**

A *It would be better not to try if you really think they're going to stick to their guns. Listen carefully to how they talk about the subject and ask questions about how receptive they would be to doing things another way. Then make a decision either to advocate the new technique or to abandon that tactic and use the weakness mitigation process instead.*

38

Is there anything you want to ask me?

This often comes near the end of the interview. If everything's gone well then make sure you don't at this point snatch defeat from the jaws of victory. On the other hand, if you think there's a problem, here's a good opportunity to go back into an area where you think they have doubts about you.

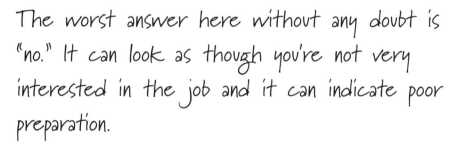

The worst answer here without any doubt is "no." It can look as though you're not very interested in the job and it can indicate poor preparation.

By this time you ought to be having a reasonable and interesting discussion with good rapport. So give two answers to this question: an open question that keeps the discussion going and a closed or more specific question that will elicit more insight into what it's like working for these people. After all, there are two decisions to be made here: They make the first decision, whether to offer you the job; then you have to decide whether to work for them.

Here's an idea for you...

You can strengthen most of the questions you want to ask by using your research. If, for example, you've read the recent press about the company you can ask the competition question much better. "I understand your main competitor is X. Is that right and who do you feel are the main players making progress in the industry?"

MORE ABOUT THE INDUSTRY AND THEIR POSITION IN IT

Start by illustrating your preparation. Use something as up to date as possible. "I'd like to hear a bit more about the industry and your position in it. There was an interesting piece in the *Times* about this Christmas being the worst for the retail industry for ten years, despite the fact that overall sales increased by 2.5 percent. Can you explain that and how do you see the next few years for retail generally?" You may think that question a bit too specific if, for example, you think they might struggle with the first part. So go even more open. "This industry has been very successful for a while now. How do you see it maintaining that progress?" This should get one or two of them going and you will listen and show that you're learning.

Another good area to probe around at this time is their competition. It's good to join an organization that recognizes it's in competition and that most companies in their industry have strengths and weaknesses. (Be careful here. Don't let yourself down by looking as though you know nothing about their industry. If you've prepared this question, don't ask it if the ground has already been covered.)

"Who do you regard as your main competition and who do you see becoming a bigger threat in the future?" It's a great idea to ask a question that's broader than the job itself. For example, if the job's international, ask something about the worldwide performance or strategy. The point is to show your interest in the future as well as the present.

AND SPECIFICALLY . . .

Be careful. Silly as it may seem, this simple question has sunk more strong interviews than many more sinister-sounding salvos. Don't focus too much on salary reviews, promotion prospects, type of car you get, parking spaces, and so on. If there are important questions you want answers to, by all means ask them. Make sure, however, that you don't look as though these things are all that's important to you: Ask some softer questions about the environment in which you'll be working. "If you had to sum up in a few words the type of person who likes working here and the type of person who fits in well, what would they be?"

You can always turn a dual question back on them: "What would you say are the main benefits of working for your organization and the main frustrations?" "Can I ask you if you have any reservations about my suitability for the job that we could discuss at this stage?" "I am applying for other positions; but I'm particularly interested in this one. Is it possible to tell me when you'll make a decision?"

Final note: Don't look as though your one and only reason for wanting to join them is to make money!

IDEA 32, *Why do you want to work for this company?*, talks about the research you need to do before attending an interview.

Try another idea...

"Holding hands at midnight
'Neath a starry sky,
Nice work if you can get it,
And you can get it if you try."
IRA GERSHWIN, songwriter

Defining idea...

How did it go?

Q **This chapter emboldened me. It made me feel that in previous interviews I'd been too meek in questioning them about why I should work for them. So when they asked this question I simply said, "Why should I come and work for you?" One person spluttered a bit and then went over some ground that we'd already covered. The other one said, "Isn't that a bit of an arrogant question?" I backpedaled madly, saying that I hadn't meant to be arrogant and that maybe I'd phrased the question wrong. It was OK in the end, but I felt I'd given way when perhaps I shouldn't have. Anyway I got the job. What do you make of all that?**

A *You probably overstepped the line a touch by asking the question so brusquely. Always remember that they are in the driver's seat because they're doing the hiring. Ask the same question with a softer touch: "What would you say are the main reasons why people like working for your organization?"*

Q **With the best will in the world I'm not going to read the *Financial Times* every day on the off-chance there will be something useful in it. What can I do instead?**

A *You can search the website of a financial newspaper or any investment website that tracks the performance of the company you're interested in. That way it'll take only a couple of minutes to find the latest published news about a company.*

39

Tell me about a time you generated a creative solution to a problem

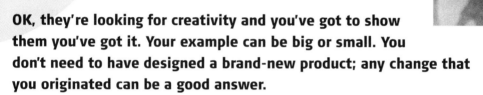

OK, they're looking for creativity and you've got to show them you've got it. Your example can be big or small. You don't need to have designed a brand-new product; any change that you originated can be a good answer.

Always look for the benefits to your organization and its customers.

Managers who succeed normally have creativity as a key attribute. Being "creative" simply means having a good idea and implementing it. It's also about not accepting things as they are because, "That's the way we've always done it." So the quick answer to the question for most people has to be, "Yes, I made something happen."

THINK HARD AND USE OBSERVATION

Here are two examples, one where a fact of life seemed to limit the business that a small retail outlet could do, and the other an example of watching people's behavior and coming up with a neat idea.

Here's an idea for you... **Look at the way you do your job from a customer's point of view. Look at all the processes involved. It's almost certain that something could be improved that you could suggest. Now sell your suggestion to your boss and you've made progress for your organization and gotten a simple but good example of creativity for your next interview.**

"After I'd been the manager of the ladies' boutique for two months, I was thinking about the peaks and dips that the business went through. It was quite simple. During the weekend we were very busy and had two extra people in. During the week we were fairly dead. But nevertheless we had to provide our service every day of the week. I started to think about what else we could use the premises for during the week. We served coffee; we stayed open at lunch. It seemed nothing more could be done. Then I saw the new trend for nail parlors, and put two and two together. I did a deal with a nearby businesswoman who agreed to use our shop as a parlor two and a half days a week. The combination of the two worked and we made a little money out of the nail service itself, but more importantly we raised clothes sales by 20 percent. We also think that we'll improve customer loyalty, since the customers who use the service love it: Once someone is in the habit of getting their nails done regularly, we get a regular selling opportunity."

Our second example features a good creative observer: "I work in fashion accessories. My friend and I had been laughing at all the women rummaging around in their handbags when their cell phones rang—and as often as not failing to get to it before it stopped ringing. I suggested to my company that we sew a special pocket into our top-range handbags to carry a phone. Women immediately saw the benefit of the simple feature. They even saw the financial benefit of not having to call everyone back all the time. The company saw a lift in sales as women traded up to the more expensive range."

AND IT COULD BE YOU

You can be in any job you want and still be creative: "I run the induction training for my company. Because of the nature of our business, health and safety takes up most of the training time. It struck me that new trainees were well-versed in health and safety but knew almost nothing about our customers when they went into the field. I suggested we do something about this to my boss, and she thought it a good idea and asked me to come up with a plan. In the end I got one or two customers to come and talk to the trainees and answer questions. It worked very well. I've had very good feedback from the trainees. The customers I involved were very impressed, and staff were able to deal with customers from day one rather than handing them over to more experienced people. My boss thinks that this idea has played a part in improving sales." So, it has to be your initiative, it must be a fresh approach, and there have to be benefits to company and customers.

An optimist is bound to be better at suggesting improvements than a pessimist. Look at IDEA 46, *Is your glass half-empty or half-full?*

Try another idea...

"You can't stop. Composing's not voluntary, you know. There's no choice, you're not free. You're landed with an idea and you have the responsibility to that idea."
HARRISON BIRTWISTLE, British composer

Defining idea...

How did it go?

Q **I was asked, "What problems occur in doing your job, and what are you doing about them?" I decided to take this as a creativity question and used a story in which I'd seen a problem at work and come up with an innovative solution. I told the truth, which involved saying that the idea had cost some money but everyone had been delighted. I was a bit shocked when the interviewer said, "So you think it's worth changing things, even if it costs money off the bottom line to do it?" Why didn't it work for me?**

A *First of all, it was a good idea to take the question the way you did. This question can expose weakness when people talk about a problem without showing that they're doing something about it. Perhaps you didn't need to talk about the cost if you couldn't offer compensating benefits. Perhaps you could have made a stronger case for the benefits and only mentioned costs if asked.*

Q **My best example was an idea that looked as though it would be of huge benefit to the company; but circumstances changed and we abandoned it. It was a neat piece of lateral thinking. Can I use it?**

A *Probably the best way to use it is to precede it with a less spectacular innovation that yielded bottom-line results. Then you can talk more confidently about the big one.*

40

How important to you is your work–life balance?

The answer to this is important, as much to you as it is to them. Make sure you do know what that balance should be before you go in. Here's a way of figuring that out—plus some suggestions to make them love your answer.

There's no point in just being a safe pair of hands for the job. That just puts you up with the others. Add some flair and evidence to your answers and you'll stand out.

Everyone is going to say that they're indeed looking for a balance and that their partner/children/interests/blah, blah, blah are important as well as their career. Here's a quick process that'll help you to know what you really want and at the same time give you an interesting way of answering the question.

WORK OUT YOUR STARTING POINT

There are 168 hours in the week, of which you spend about 56 in bed. This leaves 112 for living. Draw a three-by-three matrix of nine square boxes and write an activity

Here's an idea for you...

We're going to come across a number of questions where your research will be much improved if you have a friendly contact in the organization you are interviewing for. This is one of them. Question them about the culture of the organization and its attitude to work–life balance. It's very valuable to have that information before you go in.

heading in each of them. The headings will include some of the following: friends, relationships, family, alone time, personal development, health, hobbies, leisure, creativity, work, and any other areas of life that you enjoy or endure. If you need more squares just add them. Don't forget to add areas in which at the moment you do nothing but which you wish to get involved in.

Now list the number of hours in a typical week you spend in each of these areas, convert it to a percentage of 112 and write the percentage in the appropriate box.

That's your starting point. You may wish to check what you have written with your partner and a work colleague to make sure you're not indulging in wishful thinking. If the percentages are just what you want, well done; you just have to think through how to tell the interviewer this.

One person who did this exercise decided that he was spending too many hours watching television and too many hours working. The box that suffered from this was the one marked "wife and family." He resolved therefore to switch the TV off between Monday and Thursday. He told his boss he was only going to work late three evenings a week and that he was leaving each Wednesday and Friday at five o'clock. He started to take his wife out for dinner once a month and told his two sons that every other weekend they could have half a day of his time to do anything they wanted to do provided it didn't cost more than twenty dollars. He actually implemented a plan that was OK with his boss and delightful for his family.

There's more on this subject in **IDEA 31, *How ambitious are you?***

Try another idea...

PLAN THE SITUATION FOR THE FUTURE

Now look at the areas where you want to make adjustments. For every area whose percentage you increase you have to make a choice about which area you are going to reduce. Add in any activities that currently you don't do but have resolved to get started on. Now convert the percentages into hours and see if you believe you have a feasible plan.

That's the exercise. Now turn it into a brilliant answer to the question. It's probably a good idea to suggest you've gone through such a process. Tell them what the answer is. Watch their faces, though; some of them may be workaholics and think that's the only way for an ambitious person to be. Add a safety-first rider like, "I think that when anyone starts a new job they probably have to work a lot of hours to get it under control; if necessary during that time I'll work all the hours you need." You can also point out that people who achieve a good work–life balance tend to be more effective at work. It's not just the hours you work; it's your attitude toward getting things done.

"It is impossible to enjoy idling thoroughly unless one has plenty of work to do."
JEROME K. JEROME, British essayist

Defining idea...

How did
it go?

Q **I'm trying to change my work–life balance away from work. That's why I'm applying for this new job. I'd like to work less than forty hours per week—thirty-five, if possible. Is this an acceptable reply?**

A *It has to be, really. If they don't know and hire you, then either or both of you are going to be disappointed. Careful how you word it, though. You're trying to look like a person who makes a good contribution at work but has other important things to do, not a work-shy slacker.*

Q **I'm trying to get a promotion in a company I already work for. The team I'm trying to join is in the habit of going for a drink after work most days. Quite honestly, I don't like that and would prefer to use that time in other ways. Should I tell them?**

A *Ah, no. When you join you'll find it easy enough to join them from time to time without it becoming an uncomfortable habit. We would put this time firmly in the work part of the matrix, join them to keep up with the internal politics, and slip out when it becomes idle chatter. But there's no need to explain all that in the interview.*

41

What gets you up in the morning?

Your response here reveals a lot about you. Think about the main points you're trying to make about yourself and this job. Show how you've spent time and energy in creating what for you is an ideal working environment.

Answer with a big smile, look as though you're enjoying answering this question, and perhaps indicate that it's a lot of things in combination that add up to a happy working life.

Companies, particularly their HR departments, know that people who come to work with enthusiasm spread their enthusiasm to other people. They also know that performance is much improved when people enjoy the time they're at work. So they're looking for the kind of person who generates such a mood.

Here's an idea for you...

This is a very good question to role-play as practice with a friend or colleague. Role-play is a powerful tool for preparation work. It's extraordinary how much easier it is to field a question if you've tried it out the previous day. When you prepare an answer in your head, you tend to leave loose ends that you might not be entirely sure how to finish off in real life. Role-play forces you to face these and tie them off. It's great if you can find someone who knows the interviewer to enact their part.

LOOK FOR A FOCUS

Consider how your skills, training, and experience focus on this job. Let's imagine that the interviewers are looking mainly for a good team leader, someone with good customer-relationship skills as well as a professional technician. The answer comes out a little like this: "Nowadays, I'd say it's the team. We're working well together now. We lost the one person who I felt was holding us back from making the team something much bigger than the sum of the parts. Since then morale has just climbed. The feedback I'm getting on their pride in being in the team is terrific. I'm even getting it from people in other teams who have noticed the change."

That answer would probably lead to the question: "You sound as though you turned this team around. How did you do it?" "Using a simple activity really. When I arrived, people felt as though they had no part in any decision-making process. There was no formal way of consulting them and they didn't feel it was part of their job to knock on a door and make a suggestion. I used the 'doughnut technique' I'd learned from a great team leader I'd worked for. Every Monday morning at 8:15 a.m. I bring doughnuts into the office for everyone in the team—engineers, admin, secretaries, the lot. They knew it was going to happen so they all started to be there on time. For half an hour we discussed items on a short agenda and then for the last fifteen minutes we took any other business. Believe me, that could go anywhere. That was the start. People started to feel a sense of pride in being part of the team."

Another version of this is found at IDEA 30, *How do you manage projects?*

Try another idea...

Another good answer about your motivation: "I'm really energized when I know that what I'm doing is making a real difference."

YOU CAN FACE OUTWARD AND STILL BE METICULOUS

"Another thing that I really enjoy is the customer-facing part of the job. I enjoy meeting customers and they sure do their part to make our lives interesting. There's always something new to think about and new people to deal with. Finally, I'm motivated by the complex project side of things. We're at the leading edge with a number of our customers and we have to make some very complicated decisions and come up with innovative ways of solving problems. I've always liked that."

Expect a supplementary question on that last part: "Are you still heavily involved in the technical details of the projects in your area?" To which you might answer, "I try not to be. I've got an excellent team who can handle that side of things. We have a standing joke that my product knowledge is sketchy and they tease me that I'm out of date. I still get my hands dirty from time to time, though, and I think they know that if I have to get into the detail I can still do it."

"Awake, my soul, and with the sun Thy daily stage of duty run. Shake off dull sloth, and joyful rise, To pay thy morning sacrifice."
THOMAS KEN, British divine

Defining idea...

How did it go?

Q   **I tried role-play with an old friend. It didn't really work. To begin with I felt nervous and under pressure. Then it just didn't feel real. I'm sure I would've done better in real life than in the role-play. I'm not going to do it again because I think it might lower my confidence. Do you think that's the right decision for me?**

A   *You're absolutely right to say that you'll be better in real life than during practice. That's always the case—ask an actor. The point is that the practice makes you concentrate on the content of your answers and get some feedback. Now that you've gotten over the worst of the nervousness try the same role-play again and we bet you anything you do it better.*

Q   **I'm a salesperson and they're always trying to make me role-play although I keep telling them that I'm no good at role-play. They catch me saying things I wouldn't actually say to a real customer. Isn't it too artificial an environment?**

A   *Our experience is the opposite of what you've just said. People do say to customers what they say in role-play; it's just that most customers are too polite to point out the mistakes that employees make. We've found a huge correlation between a successful performance in role-play and successful performance in real life. If you're still reluctant to do it, you can get some of the benefit by role-playing both sides yourself, as long as you articulate both parts aloud.*

42

Tell me about yourself

This is an open question that can go anywhere. You may have to ask a clarifying question to make sure that you talk about the angle they're looking for.

Keep your answer succinct and ask frequently if you're covering the areas they want you to.

They may ask this question to open the interview, because it can expose underpreparation. The first thing to do is ask whether they want to hear about you the person or you in the context of your work. We'll take the former line and assume they answer with a question like, "Take you the person first; what are you like?"

WHAT I LIKE ABOUT LIFE

This question allows you to use some well-prepared words and to try to settle in after a nervous start. (They don't want someone who's just as stressed at the end of the interview as they were at the beginning.) You should plan also to ask open questions in return so that your response develops into a conversation.

Probably the best structure for this centers on what you like and don't like. Match this approach to the personal attributes you think they're looking for. If the job

Here's an idea for you...

When you've decided what to say about yourself, talk it over with someone who knows you well. Remind them they've got to say what they really think or they could be doing more harm than good. Look up the results of any aptitude, personality, or other tests you've done. Try to be consistent with what these told you about yourself. Such results also add credibility to the answers you give.

specification includes the terms "innovation" and "customer-facing skills" you might try something like, "My starting point would be to say that I like solving problems. From my youngest days with LEGOs, when I preferred to design as well as build the models I made, to my passion for crosswords to the new challenge of bringing up children, I like to figure out how to do things I've never done before. I'm not so happy when I have to go through routines there's no real possibility of changing. My husband points out that I can spend hours going through a yard sale to find pictures and books, but that I seem reluctant to spend a shorter amount of time doing the weekly supermarket shopping."

Don't forget that they'll probe for the weakness in such a reply: "Does this mean that you let the chores of work, like the administration and documentation, get behind?" Answer this in a reassuring way: "I know the importance of keeping my paperwork up to date and I always ensure that I'm on top of it."

Defining idea...

"Personal relationships are the thing for ever and ever, and not this outer life of telegrams and anger."
E. M. FORSTER

An alternative gambit might be, "I enjoy meeting new people. I'm sometimes a little nervous when I go into a situation where I'm with a lot of people I don't know, but I get over it fast. I often find myself being the one who introduces people and brings new people into conversations. I can stand my own company for a while, but I'm a very social animal."

NATURE VERSUS NURTURE

To get to know you more deeply, the interviewer may ask, "Do you think there are born salespeople/leaders/managers, or do you believe that you can train anyone to do these jobs?" Just hit the balance: "It's a little of both really. If you take very naturally to selling, it's important to remember that there's still a lot to learn. No one's born knowing the theory and practice of sales technique, but some people are better at implementing the theory once they've been taught it."

"Some people do seem to be naturally inclined to be leaders in any given situation. But there's a lot more to it than that. The skills involved in leadership need to be learned and practiced. I really believe the old cliché that when it comes to leadership: 'You're never too old to learn.'"

The more work-oriented version of this question is covered in IDEA 29, *Talk me briefly through your history.*

Try another idea...

"The meeting of two personalities is like the contact of two chemical substances: If there is a reaction, both are transformed."
CARL JUNG

Defining idea...

Q **On my last interview I kept tripping up on questions like this. Whatever I said, and however I proved the benefit of that personality trait, she would always ask a question about the downside of it. I found myself continuously off-balance. How should I have tackled that?**

How did it go?

A *This is not all bad. Interviewers want to test your resilience to assertive questioning and this is a good way for them to do it. It's not too important if you get a little tongue-tied—unless you haven't thought out what the* *downside might be. Next time try to preempt at least half of the supplementary downside questions in your answer.*

Q **I talked about my drive and energy, as well as how outgoing a person I am. I slowly realized that I was describing a person exactly the opposite of the person who was interviewing me. I battled on regardless. Was that the right thing to do?**

A *Not entirely. You needed to switch some of your answer to compliment the interviewer on their personal attributes. Emphasize your contemplative side and assure them of your great respect for thinkers and planners. It's just social skill, really, to reflect your personality in a way that suits the person who's listening.*

Q **In a conversation in this area, the interviewer suddenly asked about my personal interests outside work. My instinct was that it was none of her business, and I answered the question badly. Do I have to answer this question?**

A *'Fraid so. The question may elicit some useful information about you. Give a straight answer but try to incorporate some benefit to the work context. "I help with an extra reading class for children on Saturdays. It's certainly taught me patience and tolerance; and I love doing it."*

43

What's your style of influencing people?

This is kind of a trick question. The good team leader can change their style of influencing to suit the person they're working with.

You're likely to have a core style. Illustrate that and then illustrate how you can change it when necessary.

There's another angle to this question, like the Russian doll within the Russian doll. When you're in an interview, you are at that time trying to influence the interviewer. So make sure that the way you present the answer to this question reflects the demeanor and behavior of the person you're addressing.

IT'S WHAT YOU SAY

Tell them outright why no single style will fit everyone: "The main thing I've learned about influencing people is that they're all subtly different and, though most people have a natural style, everyone has to be flexible to fit. I naturally have a consultative style, influencing people by discussion and joint planning. But it comes

Here's an idea for you...

Another angle to this question concerns learning styles. Some people learn by jumping in at the deep end and doing something; others prefer to reflect long and hard before they act. Some people look very pragmatically at what works and doesn't work, while others want to understand all the theory behind what they're learning. Look around and think about the learning style of the people you work with. You could get some useful insights into how to manage them and a strong answer to questions about management style. There's lots of material on this: just search the web for "learning styles."

out differently for different people. For example, my influence over one member of my team consists almost entirely of listening to her as she works out what needs to be done and how to do it. With another person I find I have to spell things out much more, making suggestions and giving advice. Then there's another person who's very process-oriented. I motivate and influence him by facilitating a decision-making or other business process."

A little theory might come in handy: "A lot depends on the circumstances as well. Some people talk about 'push and pull' management styles; 'push' being the 'Do what you are told' or autocratic method, 'pull' the consulting democratic way of leading people. I naturally lean toward pull, but when the chips are down I can switch into being more directive if events demand it."

Then look at why people do things: "I always try to remember that people work for money but do a bit more for recognition, praise, and reward. If I think someone is doing a good job I never forget to tell them. I show appreciation often. I find it best not to wait for the end of a task to say thanks. I don't find this too difficult. I'm genuinely interested in how people work and can normally figure out how to get the best out of them."

What about creativity? "Sometimes I like to hold back from influencing the team about a decision they're making. If I'm too involved in getting them to do what I think is best, I run the risk of stifling their creativity. If I let them do it, they come up with the most amazing insights."

Working with your boss is covered in IDEA 34, *How easy are you to work with?*

Try another idea...

AND HOW YOU SAY IT

We've said that you're trying to influence the person on the other side of the desk. You have very little time to make up your mind how to do it. Some of it is quite obvious. If they behave formally, going dryly through a logical process and asking clipped questions, it's plainly inappropriate to slouch, crack jokes, or comment widely outside the answer to the question. If the person is very informal you can be more relaxed, and converse with them on their terms. (Don't go too far; you're trying to look like a professional businessperson, not a stand-up comic.)

"To the ordinary working man, the sort you would meet in any pub on Saturday night, Socialism does not mean much more than better wages and shorter hours and nobody bossing you about."
GEORGE ORWELL

Defining idea...

It's obviously much easier to get the formal/informal balance right if you've found out about the person before the start of the interview. In all cases it's hugely important to smile, thank them for what they say and do, thank them for good questions, and use their name a lot in your responses.

How did it go?

Q **My natural style is very low-key and consultative. I'm going for an interview with a guy who makes Genghis Khan look like a therapist. He is highly autocratic, to say the least. Should I say what I feel, or say that I'm more directive than I really am?**

A *A bit of both, really. Your low-key and consultative answer will still work, but you need to put a bit more emphasis on your ability to get people to take direction. Take as an example a situation where you had to take control fast, like a firing or a furious customer. Remember that the guy might actually want someone with a very different style from his own. You never know.*

Q **I had two people in the interview, one very stiff and formal and the other rather slovenly and very friendly. Should I have treated them differently?**

A *Yes. It's quite possible to alter how you answer a question according to who asked it. But it's probably safer to err on the formal side. The more relaxed person is more likely to understand that you're doing it to stay on the good side of Mr. Formality. Mr. Formality may hold it against you if you're too friendly with the other person.*

44

Your resumé says you took control when the project manager was sick. How did that go?

You must make your resumé entirely consistent with what the interviewers will discover in the interview. If you try to fool them, they'll almost certainly trip you up.

This is a simple deal breaker. If they catch you in a gross exaggeration or a lie, then you've probably blown it.

It's time to talk about bullshit. Take the example in the title of this Idea. If you've genuinely taken over for a significant length of time, then the statement is fair enough and you'll be able to substantiate it during the interview. If, however, the project manager had a couple of days off twice during the project, and you stood in for him at a couple of meetings, then your resumé is misleading. The most you can claim is, "I stood in from time to time for the project manager." Think of the

Go over your resumé with a fine-tooth comb. Challenge yourself to substantiate every claim you've made. If you feel that funnel questioning will trip you up, change the wording. You won't necessarily weaken your case and you remove the risk of looking as though you were trying to pull the wool over their eyes.

term "water cooler hero," when a junior member of a project tries to exaggerate their role by relying on the conversations the senior people had around the water cooler to bluff their way through.

THE FUNNEL TECHNIQUE

The way experienced interviewers expose such talk is to use the funnel technique. They stay very friendly as they ask one follow-up question after another until your cover is blown. It's extraordinary how often people fall for this.

"I see it says on your resumé that you measured the return on investment of sales campaigns before you submitted the proposal to the customer. How did that work?"
"Well, I had to figure out the rate of return, taking into account the value of the sale and the costs involved in production, delivery, and installation. It had to be at least 15 percent for me to be able to go ahead."
"Was that just direct costs or overheads as well?"
"I'm not sure what you mean by that."
"OK, let's talk about the rate of return.

Defining idea...

"O what a tangled web we weave When first we practice to deceive."
SIR WALTER SCOTT

Did you do a cash flow and discount it, or how did you calculate it?"
"Well, actually it was the accountants who figured it out."
"I see. What does a rate of return of 15 percent actually mean in your company?"
"Um, it was something to do with profitability."
"Yes, of course. I understand. Next, please."

The key is to be able to substantiate every statement you make on your resumé and under questioning. They're never going to take big claims at face value; they're always going to squeeze you down the funnel as they go from wide open questions to more and more specific questions.

IDEA 3, *What's your type?*, gives the detail of how to write a resumé.

Try another idea...

MAKE SURE THAT WHAT THEY'VE SEEN IS WHAT THEY GET

Your resumé covers not only what you've done in your life but also how you behave and what you're like. Your behavior in the interview has to reflect that pen portrait. So, don't give yourself an impossible task by describing a person you cannot be. If you describe yourself as energetic and enthusiastic, that's how you must act. If you talk about your careful analysis of situations before you make decisions then you should be very thoughtful in answering their questions. If you think that they're looking for an outgoing personality for the job, then by all means write down that you have that quality—as long as you can quickly overcome any nervousness at the beginning and hit a good conversational stride.

When you're checking your resumé, make sure that nothing that you've written could trip you up. Look out for adjectives; they're the words that trigger further questions. "What exactly were the *tangible* benefits?" If you've described yourself as professional you've got to look and act the part. If you've written "experienced coach and mentor," be prepared to discuss not only what you did but also the benefits to the person and the organization of the coaching that you did.

"You told a lie, an odious damnèd lie: Upon my soul, a lie, a wicked lie!"
WILLIAM SHAKESPEARE

Defining idea...

How did it go?

Q **I'm leaving a company that is going through some very high-profile problems with financial and quality issues. The division I'm in has actually not done too badly. In fact, my part of the organization made a good profit until it took on some of the costs of other divisions to make the whole look better. Can I explain that, or will I just look as though I'm being shifty, when everyone knows about the parent company's problems?**

A *You should be OK telling the truth. Have as much information to substantiate what you're saying as you think does not breach confidentiality. People do realize that not every part of a company's awful when that company has problems.*

Q **I'm only twenty and when I went through my resumé with your advice in mind I had to tone a lot down and cut some out. It looks very thin now. Don't you think I should risk some slight exaggeration? Won't it look as though I haven't done much, which could be worse?**

A *Leave it as the truth. It's much more risky to bluff. To be honest, no one has done much at your age anyway.*

45

Is it all right if we check your references now?

The days when employers didn't bother to check references are long over. There are some references who you can use and some who you must.

References are slightly dangerous things. They're unlikely to get you the job, but they could lose you it. So think them through carefully.

There is, of course, only one answer to this question. Take it as a buying sign. The interviewers are not going to check references of people they've already decided not to take. So smile confidently. "Yes, that's fine. They're aware that you might be getting in touch with them."

USE THE QUESTION AS LEVERAGE

There are some circumstances when you can demur from giving references' names—where you're applying for a job without your current employer knowing about it, for example; or where you don't want a reference to know to whom you're applying unless it's extremely likely that you'll join them.

Here's an idea for you...

If you haven't already done so, make a list of potential references and get in touch with them. Ask them to write letters of recommendation. You'll probably find that some of them, if not all, will agree to discuss what you want them to put in the document before they write it. This is very useful, since you can use them to back up the main points you're going to make when you're answering the question, "Why should we offer you this job?"

In both these cases you can use the request as an opportunity to test the water and push them along: "Yes, of course, I'm happy for you to check references; but I don't want to alert my two main references that we're talking unless we've made good progress and there's a good chance that we might be going ahead together. I wonder if this is the right time, or if you think we should wait for a bit?"

With regard to your current employer you can go even further: "I would prefer to give my current employer as a reference only when you have made me an offer that I have accepted. We should also have agreed on a start date so that I can resign in a professional way and leave a good taste behind me when I leave."

WHO DO YOU USE?

There's one reference you must use and that's your previous or current boss. If you don't, the skeptical interviewer will fear the worst. So even if they've moved on, track them down and get them to agree to act. In fact, whenever you move jobs, or start to apply for another one, speak to your boss about a reference. Ask them what they would say. Everybody knows how important it is, so most reasonable people will not only tell you what they will say but might even write it down there and then and show you.

It's a good idea to gather a few of these recommendations as your career progresses so that you can pull out a bunch of good opinions whenever someone asks for one.

The best way to be confident about any reference is to get an advance copy of what they would say in a general recommendation and to get them to copy you on the one they actually send in response to the organization's request. Frequently, this is on a pre-prepared form.

IDEA 34, *How easy are you to work with?*, looks at interviewers who might encourage you to say something negative about your current boss.

Try another idea...

A slightly quirky, and often excellent, reference is someone who has worked for you rather than the other way around. They'll say something about what it's like to work for you and what they liked about it.

If you're looking for your first job, it's still best to have someone for whom you've done some work. The shop manager where you had your Saturday job or the warehouse you worked at during college vacations will do pretty well. If there really isn't anyone who you've worked for (not even as a babysitter?) you might have to fall back on personal references. Human resources departments are not terribly impressed with personal references, since you can choose the one you want as opposed to having to choose one from your working past.

When you're talking to a potential reference, remember the three areas you want them to comment on:

- Leadership: your drive, energy, and self-insight
- Job function: your technical capabilities in doing the job
- Future potential: your relationships with others and your ambition for the future

"You will find it a very good practice always to verify your references, sir!"
MARTIN JOSEPH ROUTH, British classicist

Defining idea...

How did
it go?

Q   **I don't quite understand this. I'm in a very delicate situation. I'm applying to the main competitor of the company I work for. I don't know what my employer would do if I, or the company I'm applying to, let them in on the secret. So I thought it was good advice to say that I wouldn't give them the reference until we had agreed when I would start. Doesn't that mean that my current employer's reference is irrelevant?**

A   *It could be. But more likely is that your potential new employer will make the offer dependent on getting satisfactory references.*

Q   **I want to use a recommendation that I got from a summer job employer a year ago. Subsequently, he discovered that some of the students who worked for him had been taking time off and doing much less than he had thought. He's painting us all with the same brush although I've assured him that I wasn't among the slackers. Is it dangerous to use the old recommendation?**

A   *I'm afraid so. If the interviewer gets in touch with the man having seen his recommendation and gets a different story from him at that time, it could be serious enough for them to stop considering you. Rack your brains and think of someone else.*

46

Is your glass half-empty or half-full?

For most interviewers a positive mental attitude is almost an obsession. Find a way of displaying yours, and talk about the difference it can make.

It's true that the attitude with which we approach events does have an impact on how things turn out.

If we wish to perform at our best and to help others do the same we need to start from the attitude that everyone is equipped with the ability to succeed. Now, how do you get that into the answer to an interview question?

WE CAN MAKE IT HAPPEN

What's behind this question is a rather negative probe. The supplementary questions are likely to be in the area of how you handle setbacks and how you behave when things are not going as well as they might. So start with a huge smile

Here's an idea for you...

Take a task that you have to perform and that you are not looking forward to. First, remember that it is your choice whether or not to do the task. Now imagine having completed the task, and that you enjoyed doing it. Next, set aside the time to do the task—the sooner the better. Choose to be positive about the job rather than downbeat. If you start off feeling negative it will make the task much more of a chore you can't enjoy. Try it; it works.

and an assurance that you are naturally a very positive person. Then use an example of someone you have known who passes that attitude on to others. Try to give examples of what they did, to show that the attitude comes out in real activities as opposed to anything that's pie in the sky.

"At heart I'm definitely an optimist. I've worked with both types of people. I've worked with a team leader who was a terrible pessimist and moaner. He was always criticizing the company and the people in it. I had to keep reminding myself that nothing was as bad as he was making it out to be; but some people in the team got infected with the glass-half-empty bug, and didn't enjoy their work. I know our performance suffered as a result. I've also worked with a woman who was the opposite. She refused to use the word 'problem,' and put messages on the board saying, for example, that 'I can't' or 'we can't' were both banned phrases. We all expected to succeed in her environment and we did."

This is an area where an analogy with sports can be useful: "It's interesting when you consider sports. There's an obvious phenomenon that champion teams win even when they're not playing very well. I think it's something to do with the fact that they're simply expecting to win. The 'positive mental attitude' that sports coaches talk about does have an effect."

AND WHEN THE GOING GETS TOUGH?

A person who expects everything to go right at work is not an incurable optimist so much as a fool. They'll probe for your response to adversity. "How do you handle rejection?" This is particularly asked of customer-service people in a competitive industry. If they can't handle losing a few then they should be in another profession: "I think that being rejected from time to time is part of the process of being a salesperson. After all, if every customer said 'yes' the company wouldn't need a sales force in the first place. I try to take responsibility for a loss without taking it as a personal rejection. That way I can move on knowing that I'm one campaign closer to my next sale."

Look at this question in terms of a team with IDEA 50, *The division you'd be managing is demoralized. How will you re-motivate them?*

Try another idea...

Another way to probe for negativity is, "Why do you want to leave your job?" It's quite possible to answer this one positively, even though you are leaving because of the lack of something. Just show how there is nothing anyone can do about your reason for leaving: "It's a small business. I've learned what I can from it and there is no advancement possible." Or: "The job was interesting when I started, and I've enjoyed doing it and being successful; but I think the time has come to tackle something more challenging."

"You've got to ac-cent-tchu-ate the positive
Elim-my-nate the negative
Latch on to the affirmative
Don't mess with Mr. In-between."
JOHNNY MERCER, songwriter

Defining idea...

How did
it go?

Q **I tried a positive mental attitude and it proved very intriguing. I had to take a trip to a customer that involved catching busy trains, changing twice, not being able to park at the station, and so on. And at the end of the journey I knew I would be facing a far from satisfied customer. So I tried this thing out. I imagined everything about the journey going well, and the discussion with the customer proceeding in a way that produced a very positive outcome. Guess what? It went like a dream! Isn't that amazing?**

A *Yes, it's interesting, isn't it? It's also why we put some tasks off and then find when we do tackle them that there wasn't much difficult about them at all. Anyway you've got a good story to tell the interviewer if a question like this comes up. Just one thing: Don't make it sound metaphysical or spiritual. That goes over well with some people, but others hate it.*

Q **I'm a salesman and I got the rejection question. I answered much as you suggested and a sales manager suggested that if I didn't feel bad, either I wasn't expecting success or I didn't feel that it was because of what I'd done that I didn't get the business. How should I have handled that?**

A *Perhaps you need a little introduction to your positive attitude, such as, "Well, I wouldn't be human if it didn't hurt when someone chooses not to buy; but I've learned not to let it get me down for more than a moment."*

47

What are your strengths and weaknesses?

This is a very general question that you should expect. It deserves a well-prepared answer. You need to demonstrate not only a high level of self-insight but also corroborating evidence from other people.

This is an example of a double question, often used by HR people: "What's positive about...and what's negative about...?"

For each planned assertion of a strength or weakness, think of a supplementary question they might ask. Often the real test is these supplementary questions, so you have to prepare for them.

I'M GOOD; I'M VERY, VERY GOOD

Start with a general statement of what you are and what you do. Then show what strengths you had to have to achieve the results you have: "I'm an energetic IT professional with experience in running complex projects. I have a proven record of delivering the benefits of technology to a business. I have run teams as big as thirty and have had to involve many other people in the organization in order to

Here's an idea for you...

Good interviewers are adept at getting to your strengths and weaknesses—through what they've read about you and through the interview process. It's vital, therefore, that you do have good insights into the real you. Take all of your appraisals—you have kept them, haven't you?—and list the strengths and weaknesses that the appraisers have picked out. There will be a pattern that you should take very seriously. When you've finished your preparation for this question, go over your answer with somebody senior who knows you well. You may as well have their insights, too.

implement computer projects. During that time I developed my strengths in a number of areas. First, I'm very commercially minded. I never forget that IT is there to serve the financial performance of the organization. (I've had to convert some people who start from the opposite position—that the organization is there to benefit the smooth running of the IT department.) After I delivered my last project the managing director went on record as saying that the project had saved the company millions of dollars in currency transactions.

"I have strong project management and control skills; but I recognize that all the project management tools in the world don't get the work done. People do that. I enjoy leading teams and I have skills in involving and motivating the people in them. My last boss will testify to that and two of my references are people who've been in teams I've managed. Most of the projects I've done have meant that a lot of people have had to change how they work. There's often heavy resistance to change and my tenacity when things are difficult has been fully tested. A departmental manager for whom I implemented a new system believes that I had at one point more people trying to hinder my delivering the system than I had helping me. Having said that, another strength I have is flexibility. If I have to change course I can do so rapidly in order to meet a new demand." Notice the pattern: The result, the strengths necessary to achieve that result, and finally the evidence from a third party.

Another way of putting the question is, "What would you say are your outstanding qualities?" You can probably structure your answer in a similar way. If you choose to talk more personally try not to give them a simple list. It's much stronger to pick out one or two qualities and tell a story illustrating the benefits of those particular qualities.

Another version of this question is found in IDEA 46, Is your glass half-empty or half-full?

Try another idea...

BUT IF I HAVE A WEAKNESS...

Choose weaknesses that are based on truth. Remember, they're looking for self-insight, but choose weaknesses that, in fact, will probably benefit the organization rather than hinder it: "I've discussed with my manager a couple of areas that I need to think about and work on improving. If I have a team member who's struggling with something, I tend to jump in and do the job for them if I'm not careful rather than leave them to develop their skills. I do this sometimes when time is short. I need to put in place good training and development plans to make sure I don't do this. Although I appreciate the importance of my work/life balance to both the quality of my life and my accomplishments at work, I do sometimes overbalance toward work. Both I and my family are working on this."

Finish off by using the term "weakness" in its alternative meaning to end with a little humor. "I also have a weakness for the Buffalo Bills. It's sad, I know, but I'm afraid incurable."

"O! it is excellent to have a giant's strength, but it is tyrannous to use it like a giant."
WILLIAM SHAKESPEARE

Defining idea...

How did
it go?

Q **I've looked through my old appraisals and found an inconsistency. One person talks about my strength in presentation skills, particularly my ability to think on my feet, change course if necessary, and still achieve the objective of the presentation. Someone else talking in the same area said that I relied on my presentation skills to get me out of potential problems I could possibly have avoided by doing more preparation. So, what do I do?**

A *Celebrate! You've found a double answer to the double question. Tell them about the skills as a strength, and show them that you're very careful not to take it for granted that these will get you through. You've learned that you still have to do all the preparation work to make sure.*

Q **Look, I don't suffer fools gladly. You talk as though that should be called a weakness. I intend to talk about it as a strength. Why shouldn't I?**

A *We wish you a happy life, in which you neither meet, nor work with, nor work for any fools. The rest of us try to overcome the weakness of being impatient with less competent people by working to develop their capabilities.*

48

How do you make important decisions?

They're looking for method here, checking that you've thought about decision making per se and that you look at a situation from all angles before you decide what to do.

In answering this question, never forget that a decision is not really finalized until the actions that flow from it have truly started.

It's another balancing act. On the one hand you have to be seen as making a major decision in a structured, logical way. Your process must ensure you don't, for example, miss the best option available. On the other hand, they don't want to see a love of bureaucracy that makes your decision making so process-oriented that it stifles flair and intuition. And it has to have a shortcut version that allows you to come to a rough conclusion quickly.

EXPLAINING THE PROCESS

Fundamentally, an important decision is one that affects a lot of people and/or involves a lot of money. A decision is also important if getting it wrong could have a hugely detrimental impact on the company. Explain your process and demonstrate

Here's an idea for you...

If you explain a process to the interviewer they're bound to follow up with, "Give me an example of a time when you've gone through that process." It's a good idea, therefore, to take a key decision that you or your team made and write down an analysis of this process so that you've got a great example to talk about.

that you can do it fast when necessary: "I was fortunate in being taught a decision-making process on a training course. I've modified it a bit, mainly to make sure that it doesn't take too long to reach a final decision. I find it better to go through this process with a team, but it's possible to do it on my own. We first agree what we've got to make a decision about. Then we go through four steps:

"We identify the issues, the problems or opportunities, around the topic. We take care to understand as accurately as possible the impact each issue has on performance.

"From there we move to discussing the options. This is when flair and lateral thinking are at their most effective. That's why it's so useful to do it in a team: You never know who may come up with a new option.

"When we're sure we've identified all the options, we evaluate them. I get the team to agree what the selection criteria should be. There might be a criterion that the chosen solution must require very few extra people in the team to implement it. Then we systematically mark each of the options on a scale of 1–10 on each criterion. This gives us a good measure to compare options. We can also decide which criteria are the most important to us.

"This gives a good logical platform on which to make the decision. Through bitter experience I've found that decision making must not stop there. You then have to agree on the action plan and decide who's responsible for each action. That way you make sure that your brilliant decision actually gets implemented.

"I've used this process often enough to be able to go through it quickly if I have to make a quick decision."

There's more on balanced thinking in IDEA 47, *What are your strengths and weaknesses?*

Try another idea...

They may ask, "Do you think it's important to document all this analytical work?" You reply, "Crucial; otherwise you find that you haven't tied off all the loose ends and everyone involved has a different view of the decision and how it was made. Documentation makes it possible for other people to learn from the process you went through and is useful for evaluating the decision-making process after the dust has settled."

WHAT ABOUT RISK?

"*Wherever you see a successful business someone once made a courageous decision.*"
PETER DRUCKER, management consultant

Defining idea...

If you haven't mentioned the word "risk" in your reply, it'll probably come up in a supplementary question: "How do you take risk into account?" Describe a similar process for risk analysis: "We identify everything that could go wrong in implementing the decision and estimate the probability of the risk occurring and the impact on performance if it does. This gives a quick and accurate picture of the most significant risks. The team can then agree on actions to mitigate the key risks."

"*Ever notice that 'What the hell' is always the right decision?*"
MARILYN MONROE

Defining idea...

213

How did it go?

Q **I tried this with a horrible result. I went through your process in retrospect on a decision that I and another woman took about three months ago. First we thought of some other options. Then we found that the decision we'd actually made came third in the evaluation. The interview's tomorrow so I've got to fix it. How?**

A *Take each of the criteria and weigh it, making sure that the highest weight goes to the criteria that your actual decision scored highest in. Now multiply the scores on the criteria by the weight to give the weighted average. Keep adjusting the weights until your decision soars above the rest. You'll need to have good arguments for how you chose the weights in case they ask about that, too.*

Q **When I was trying to get some more money out of the advertising director, I asked her if she agreed with how I was evaluating the decision and she said yes but that she wanted to add another criterion. This threw me, since the one she chose didn't really favor the decision I was promoting. I stuttered and stammered to try to fit the new criterion in. Isn't this going to happen quite often?**

A *Possibly, but if she had not come up with the new criterion then it would have emerged as an objection to your decision later on. Take a careful note of the new criterion and make sure you have understood exactly what the director is looking for. Then go back to your decision. You have until the end of the meeting to think about how to deal with the new issue. That's more time than you'd have had if the issue had come up as an objection.*

49

What reservations would you have if we offered you the job?

This question could offer room for negotiation. It's also a direct request for information. What you say could, of course, affect whether or not they actually make the offer.

Don't forget the rule that covers all interview answers—always start with a positive.

Tackle this in three ways: First, what you like about the job, second, a strategic reservation about taking the job, and finally, something to encourage them to make their best offer or to alter the job's conditions to your advantage.

THERE'S SOMETHING THEY CAN'T PUT RIGHT

The psychology toward the end of an interview is interesting. Both sides can start to believe that there is an exact fit: They want you to do the job, and you can't believe that this is so like the job you want. This is sometimes called the "halo effect." Don't succumb to it. Go back over the criteria you've set yourself and make sure that this job is right for you.

Here's an idea for you...

Before you go into the final interview or if they've asked you back to dot the i's and cross the t's of your offer letter, refine the detail of your criteria for taking the job. What's different between what you originally wanted and what they're offering? Is there anything else that would make the job even more perfect? The original criteria you used when deciding who to apply to and who to go and see may well be out of date. You need to have the new list firmly in your head to tackle this question to your full advantage.

"I really like what I've understood about the job from my research, my observation of what goes on here, and from the interview process. The challenge looks terrific and I'm certain I can handle it and do a good job. When I first started looking, however, I thought I would stay in the banking area at this stage in my career. It's what I've known for a while now. But I'm still very attracted to the job we're discussing."

Now you can just ask for time to think about it. After all, an offer in the hand is useful even if just as a benchmark for other possibilities: "What I've learned about the civil service has certainly changed my mind in a number of ways and perhaps that reservation is more a misunderstanding than a deal breaker." Now wait for their response. They may offer to let you have a further look around, or propose some training to fill any knowledge gap. It's useful to keep quiet at some moments and let them decide where to take the conversation.

There's another question in this area that you must not let throw you: "What do you think will be the least interesting part of the job?" The safe route is to take something that no one in any job likes doing and make a joke of it. They may not be happy about anything else that you might mention, so play the percentage shot: "Keeping the hard copy filing up to date is not my favorite time of the week; but I know it's got to be done."

IDEA 32, *Why do you want to work for this company?*, adds advice about the research you need to do in order to answer this question.

Try another idea...

If there lurks in the back of your mind a real reservation about your ability to do the job, or if you feel that in one area you've oversold your skills and knowledge, this is a good time to air the matter. The worst that can happen is that they don't offer you a job that you couldn't handle, which is no bad thing. The best that can happen is that they become aware you're going to need help or training in that area.

AND SOMETHING THEY CAN

Unless you think it's insensitive, like if you think it might wreck the euphoria of the moment, pop in a negotiable point here: "The only logistics thing that troubles me is traveling into the city every day. I had been hoping to work at home at least one day of the week." Use the moment when they're making a job offer to negotiate the best terms and conditions possible.

"I take the official oath today with no mental reservations, and with no purpose to construe the Constitution or laws by any hypercritical rules."
ABRAHAM LINCOLN

Defining idea...

How did it go?

Q **I knew that my spreadsheet skills would be under pressure in the new job, so I told the interviewers I had a reservation in that area and expressed my eagerness to get some training in the subject. Although the senior woman and the HR guy seemed OK with this, and indeed did talk about providing training, my potential boss looked unhappy. He definitely damped down the other people's enthusiasm and I thought all was lost. Eventually they all agreed that it wasn't a deal breaker; but it was a close call, so are you sure about your advice in this particular area?**

A *You've got the job and no one can say that you misled them about your spreadsheet skills, least of all your boss. You should be able to motivate him to get you some training the moment you go on board. Incidentally, are you sure you hadn't purposely or perhaps by accident suggested earlier that you knew more about spreadsheets than you do? Have a look at what your resumé hints at in this area.*

Q **If they ask me this question my only real reservation concerns the guy that I'll have to work for. He doesn't seem that smart to me. Should I find a form of words to say that to them?**

A *Possibly. You could have tried asking the question, "What are you like to work for?" This will give you more evidence. Think about life with that person. Will you be happy working there? Then make a decision, because if you express doubts about your boss's competence right from the start you're asking for trouble. Best to avoid the job if it's a big problem.*

50

The division you'd be managing is demoralized. How will you re-motivate them?

A fair and difficult question. Answer with a process to fix the immediate problems, and a plan for boosting motivation in the long term.

Remember that the members of the team are the best people to ask for ideas on how to improve matters.

This is not an uncommon situation. The team needs a new leader, perhaps because the old one didn't get them to perform their best or achieve their objectives. The new leader faces more than the normal problems of taking on a new team—wariness about a stranger and so on.

Here's an idea for you...

If you haven't facilitated a team planning session you should do so. It's extraordinary the insights such a meeting can produce. Keep it simple; start from a general statement of what the team is trying to achieve. Document the strengths, weaknesses, opportunities, and threats the team faces in achieving results. This identifies the issues the team needs to address. Set objectives for improving matters and make a clear action plan. Don't believe the naysayers who complain that strategic planning is difficult. A manager needs to be able to show experience in this area when going for a new job or promotion.

THE FIRST FEW WEEKS

Start your answer with an assurance that you'll put a lot of effort into this crucial part of your role: "I'd recognize the importance of spending a huge amount of time with the team, talking to them and getting to know them. I'd use that time to thoroughly analyze what the problems are as the team sees them; why they're not feeling good about their work."

You may then get the question, "What do you think are the likely causes of poor team morale?" You might reply, "In my experience it frequently starts from a communications problem. The team doesn't feel that management is keeping them informed. This often happens if a manager is trying not to worry a team with some problems the organization has. This never works. They're not fools and they know something's going on; so they worry, even though they don't know the details. I'd make sure as quickly as I can that they hear the full story of the organization's position and theirs in it.

"The other main cause of team demotivation is lack of involvement in the decision-making process. If their views are not taken into account when plans are made they're going to feel unhappy. I find that the best people to find a way around problems or improve a difficult situation are usually the people at the front lines. If you want to know how to sell more product and services ask the salespeople. If you need to reduce direct costs ask the people in production. I use a structured but simple team planning process that makes certain that everyone contributes to planning the way ahead." Be prepared for a supplementary question on planning processes.

IDEA 41, What gets you up in the morning?, offers more on this area.

Try another idea...

AND THEN FOREVER

"How do you keep your team wanting to come to work in the morning?" One possible answer: "I find that resolving issues quickly is best done by assigning teams of, say, two people to find solutions. This is stronger than an individual working on their own with occasional input from their leader. I also know how important a wide perspective of what's going on in the organization is to a team. I make sure they know how important they and their work are to the whole organization— that's a huge motivator. I believe that bonuses and rewards are part of motivating a team but by no means the whole of it. I understand the crucial importance of appreciating their efforts—they need regular praise and thanks. Sometimes it's good to set monthly goals so that the team can get together more frequently to celebrate their achievements. I also find that people need to get involved in new activities and new challenges."

"In order that people may be happy in their work, these three things are needed: They must be fit for it. They must not do too much of it. And they must have a sense of success in it."
JOHN RUSKIN, British critic

Defining idea...

The interviewers are unlikely to go into the specifics of what went wrong with the team, unless you're going for an internal job. In the latter case, you need to research carefully what's caused the demoralization.

How did it go?

Q **When I suggested that bonuses play a part in team motivation I was asked, "Doesn't that sound like buying your way out of your duties as a leader?" What's the answer to that?**

A *The best answer is to avoid being asked that question. Perhaps you overdid the bonuses part at the expense of other types of rewards. Make sure you've put enough emphasis on appreciation and involvement. If you do get that reaction, try, "Good heavens, no! Money is only a part of motivation. You can't ignore it, but you can't rely on it to do the whole job."*

Q **When I talked about running a planning process, the interviewer told me that, if given the job, I'd have a two-day away session to do our plan, facilitated by an outside resource. She was skeptical that I could do it without that sort of resource. Are you suggesting I should be able to do what a facilitator does?**

A *Yes. You can always use the same process to review the plan during the year. You've got to be able to do this stuff, because events can occur that require a radical review of the plan at any time; events don't wait until the annual session comes along. However, if your boss offers a facilitator, take them up on it: You'll be able to give your full attention to the plan itself rather than to managing the event.*

How do you get things done?

Research shows that all successful managers are strong in two areas: general intelligence (helps you figure things out) and conscientiousness (helps you get things done). Here's a series of questions specifically about the latter.

They're going to try to pin down how hard and meticulously you work and how effective you are.

There's not a lot they can ask about your general intelligence. They'll look at your education and qualifications. They'll look at your analytical skills and judgment by asking questions about your experience and possibly give you a series of tests. That leaves us with conscientiousness.

JUST HOW EFFECTIVE ARE YOU?

"Tell me about a time when you had to work extremely hard to ensure that a project was completed." This is fairly straightforward but there's one lurking snake. Be careful that your reply doesn't make it look as though you left things to the last minute or didn't have an appropriate work plan. Taking something over would be a good example, as would responding to an external event that changed things: "I was managing the project to support the maintenance of a new product. The timescale we had planned for was fifteen months. Then a competitor brought out a similar product and the board decided to move more quickly with ours. We had to

Here's an idea for you...

Prepare at least two PERL project examples, big or small. You'll almost certainly get a question that will tee up these stories and they'll have the ingredients they're looking for: good business process and methodical implementation backed by talent, i.e., conscientiousness.

shave three months off the original plan." Lay it on thick if you can: "And it was Christmas the month before the new completion date."

Now show that you didn't just go all out, but sat down and made a plan: "I got the team together and we discussed the situation frankly and agreed we were going to go for it. We warned our families that we would be at work for a lot more time than usual and arranged for most of the team to take time off after we finished."

Now explain how the team rose to the challenge: "The team was amazing. We were so close-knit and cooperative that we completed the first pilot test on-site before the launch. What did it was terrific communication, a plan that everyone bought into, and then, well, long hard hours. Very rewarding at the end for all of us."

Notice how the team gets given the credit all the time. So that's the template: Something unexpected, a complete re-plan, thoughtfulness about the team, and success.

"Tell me about a time when you had to cut through organizational barriers." Don't make it look as though you hadn't expected the barrier. Use something unexpected again. Demonstrate what you did with your ability to get people in other departments to cooperate. But also mention some top-level support. They're not looking for someone who goes out on a limb without some sort of safety rope. Don't forget to spell out the benefit to the company of your breaking the rules.

The interviewers might ask a very straightforward question about this. See IDEA 36, *Do you enjoy hard work?*

Try another idea...

HAVING A LOT OF BALLS IN THE AIR

Conscientiousness includes juggling priorities. "Tell me about a time when you had to adjust your priorities in order to meet a new and urgent requirement." Start in the same way by making sure that the change in priorities doesn't come across as a planning problem. If you've taken the initiative, that's good: "Because sales had gone well, I realized that bringing out the top of the range before the mid-range would improve profitability." Keep it action-oriented. Yes, they want to hear there was a plan, but they also want to know what you did and how you got people to do their part.

"Tell me about the biggest goal you had to achieve last year. What steps did you take to meet that goal?" PERL is useful here: Plan, Execute, Reflect, and Learn. You made a plan, you implemented it with frequent pauses to evaluate what you were doing, and you learned a lot as the team went through the project.

"The Way of our Master is none other than conscientiousness and altruism."
CONFUCIUS

Defining idea...

225

How did it go?

Q I found PERL interesting, but it doesn't work. We work quite well as a team. I have no problems getting people together to make a plan or to monitor how the plan is being executed. But when I tried to call a meeting to reflect on what we were doing almost everyone declined because they were too busy doing things to move the project along—they were executing. How can you argue with them?

A *You need a result here. Make a couple of one-on-one meetings happen, formally or informally. Talk about the project and ask the other person for suggestions as to how you could improve the processes you're going through. In our experience they'll all come up with something and that is the point of "reflect."*

Q I left school when I was seventeen despite everyone saying I should go to college. I couldn't bear the fact that all my friends were earning money, so I got a job. I'm twenty-five now and trying to get a job in management. While I can make good arguments about my conscientiousness, will people suspect my intelligence and regard it as a barrier to my becoming a manager?

A *We only said that education was one way by which employers will seek an indication of intelligence. The work you've done will probably compensate for your lack of qualifications, but there are, we're afraid, people out there who regard a lack of qualifications as a deal breaker for senior jobs. You'll probably succeed through your endeavors and results, but maybe you should think about a relevant course that you could do at the same time as a full-time job. Many employers support their people doing this, because it's in their interests, too.*

How good are your time-management and presentation skills?

Two items that often come up in second interviews or assessment centers are inbox exercises and presentations.

Don't let the time pressure rush you into rash decisions on the inbox. Make sure you know your exact aim for your presentation.

They can simulate your inbox very dramatically nowadays, with twenty emails, your computer buzzing to signal an urgent message, and a tray overflowing with paperwork.

BE SYSTEMATIC AND BE SEEN TO BE SYSTEMATIC

Don't act on the items as they come. Make sure you've read everything before you make any decisions. There could be a snake at the bottom of the pile. It's also likely that one item will have an impact on another. The most popular way of handling this exercise is, like all great techniques, very simple. Put the paperwork and emails into three categories—A, B, C—by assessing their urgency and impact. "Urgent" is something that's got to be done or it'll be too late. "Impact" measures how much

Here's an idea for you...

It's a good idea to announce at the start of a role-play presentation exactly what you want the group to decide at the end. The audience then knows where you're going to take them. Some people avoid this, since there's a risk that someone in the audience will tell you it won't be possible to achieve your aim; but logically it is better to know this at the start of the presentation than at the end. If you know what the audience's objections are, you may be able to use the presentation to overcome them.

an item affects the profit-and-loss account or other people.

A: Stuff that you think is urgent, that in real life you would do today—things you're going to deal with during the exercise. Matters to do with customers are most likely to occupy this category.

B: Stuff that's important but not as urgent as A. You'll get around to these today only if you finish with A. Tomorrow these matters could well go into A.

C: Material that may still be important. You need to know where it is, so that if something happens that changes its urgency or impact you can promote the item to A or B.

If during the exercise they interrupt you with phone calls, establish quickly who is calling and what their position is. You'll want to speak immediately to your boss, for example, since they may well change at least one of your priorities. When these interruptions occur, make sure that an observer can see you're applying the same systematic rules to each one, and putting those that don't need action now into C, even when someone on the phone says the matter's urgent.

PRESENTATION TIPS

If you're not a natural at presentations, train until you can at least survive. Ken knows one senior manager who made it to the top and remained a complete liability on his feet. When asked how he'd survived he replied, "Ducking and weaving, old boy. I avoided presentations like the plague."

The best tips for making effective presentations are the usual suspects: Set tight objectives and talk exclusively in terms the audience will understand. The easiest way to set objectives for a presentation is to write down, At the end of this presentation the audience will:

- Do something;
- Be able to do something; or
- Have a certain attitude toward an event or plan.

This works well for an interview presentation and makes your preparation easier and quicker. In an interview, you will also have in mind the impression of you that you want to leave behind. For example: "They'll see my drive and energy, my good listening skills, and the fact that I work thoughtfully without making rash decisions."

During your preparation, try to put yourself in the audience's shoes. This should help you to use only the language that they use and understand. Don't forget when you're planning your magnificent opening that you've also got to finish with a bang. (We've both found that "Er, well, that's it" is a frequently used ending.) Allow time for questions and think through what the questions are likely to be, so you can

See IDEA 43, *What's your style of influencing people?*, for tips on persuading others.

Try another idea...

"Unless one is a genius, it is best to aim at being intelligible."
SIR ANTHONY HOPE HOSKINS, British novelist

Defining idea...

229

Defining idea...

"Presentations are about them, the audience, rather than you, the speaker."
RICHARD HUMPHREYS, British venture capitalist

respond professionally. Lots of good presentations founder at question time. Only cover the main points on the visual aids, make sure they have impact, and don't just read them. They're aids for you to talk about.

How did it go?

Q **I tried to do the ABC analysis but it went wrong. A lot of the inbox was email. I tried to add the letters A, B, or C on to the messages, but got confused and in the end missed a really important item. What should I have done?**

A *Either print out the emails or put the topic and a reference to the email on a piece of paper—or better, a spreadsheet if you're quick at making those. You can then sort the emails as you do everything else.*

Q **I was making a presentation to three people. Suddenly one of them made a point and another one bluntly disagreed with her. In no time they were at each other's throats. I tried to break in, but in the end just looked like a fool as I tried to get my voice heard. What were they doing?**

A *This is almost certainly a setup to see if they can rattle you. Stop trying to present, look appealingly at the chairperson, and, if they don't intervene, try, "We've obviously got a disagreement here. Can I suggest that we move on and talk about that later?"*

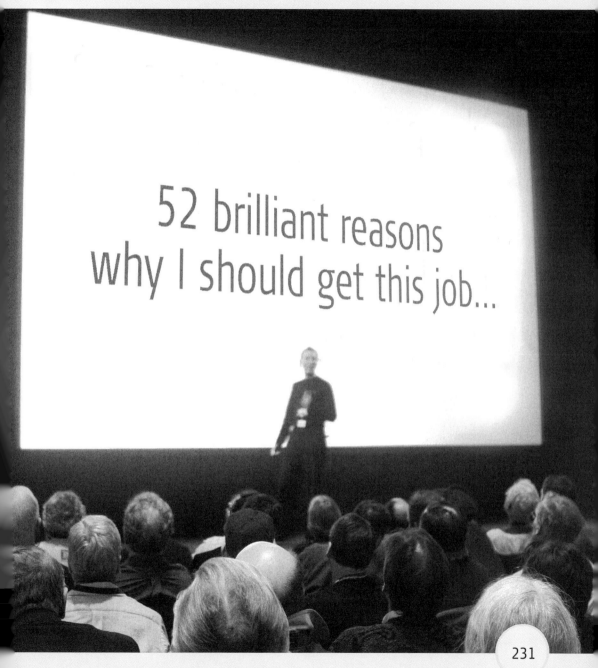

Where it's at...

Index

52 Brilliant Ideas

UNLEASH YOUR CREATIVITY
978-0-399-53325-9

LIVE LONGER
978-0-399-53302-0

SECRETS OF WINE
978-0-399-53348-8

DETOX YOUR FINANCES
978-0-399-53301-3

CELLULITE SOLUTIONS
978-0-399-53326-6

RAISING A HEALTHY EATER
978-0-399-53339-6

PERIGEE An imprint of Penguin Group (USA)

one good idea can change your life

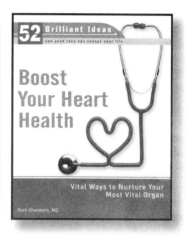